A Code of Conduct for Nuclear Command, Control, and Communication

This book presents a study of existing cases of informal international law-making and seeks to propose a code of conduct for State Nuclear Command, Control, and Communication (NC3).

As the threat of nuclear escalation rises with increasingly fractious situations in Ukraine, Taiwan, and the Middle East, the risk of accidental or illegal deployment of nuclear weapons is likewise escalating. Experts in security studies have long called for better clarification on best practice in State NC3. This study explores how each nuclear weapons State structures (and should structure) its NC3 and what international law governs nuclear operations. Given the lack of international law regarding NC3, this book argues that it would be beneficial to adopt a code of conduct or other non-binding instrument outlining any law regarding nuclear weapons operations, including any best practice regarding how States should structure their NC3 systems, given their strategic and policy objectives. In proposing a model code of conduct, this study will examine the existing literature and practice on the adoption and implementation of non-binding instruments in the international law of armed conflict, to better understand how and why non-binding instruments gain traction in State practice. The final chapter will then apply those conclusions to a draft code of conduct for State NC3.

This book will be of interest to scholars and practitioners of international law and security studies and a valuable resource for those working in the field of nuclear command, control, and communication in government and in civil society.

Emily Crawford is a professor at the University of Sydney Law School, Australia.

A Code of Conduct for Nuclear Command, Control, and Communication

Lessons from Informal International Lawmaking

Emily Crawford

Routledge
Taylor & Francis Group
LONDON AND NEW YORK

First published 2027
by Routledge
4 Park Square, Milton Park, Abingdon, Oxon OX14 4RN

and by Routledge
605 Third Avenue, New York, NY 10158

Routledge is an imprint of the Taylor & Francis Group, an informa business

British Library Cataloguing-in-Publication Data
A catalogue record for this book is available from the British Library

ISBN: 978-1-041-28412-3 (hbk)
ISBN: 978-1-041-28409-3 (pbk)
ISBN: 978-1-003-75929-4 (ebk)

DOI: 10.4324/9781003759294

Typeset in Times New Roman
by Apex CoVantage, LLC

Contents

Table of Abbreviations

AI	Artificial intelligence
API	Additional Protocol I
APII	Additional Protocol II
ARSIWA	Articles on the Responsibility of States for Internationally Wrongful Acts
DoD	US Department of Defense
DPRK	Democratic People's Republic of Korea
ENMOD	Convention on the Prohibition of Military or Any Other Hostile Use of Environmental Modification Techniques
HCoC	Hague Code of Conduct Against Ballistic Missile Proliferation
ICC	International Criminal Court
ICJ	International Court of Justice
ICRC	International Committee of the Red Cross
ICRC CIHL Study	ICRC Study on Customary International Humanitarian Law
ICTY	International Criminal Tribunal for the Former Yugoslavia
IDF	Israel Defense Forces
IHL	International humanitarian law
MTCR	Missile Technology Control Regime
NATO	North Atlantic Treaty Organization
NC3	Nuclear command, control, and communication
NCA	National Command Authority (Pakistan)
NPT	Treaty on the Non-Proliferation of Nuclear Weapons
PMSC	Private military and security companies
SIPRI	Stockholm International Peace Research Institute
SSBN	Ballistic missile submarine
TPNW	Treaty on the Prohibition of Nuclear Weapons
UN	United Nations
UNCLOS	United Nations Convention on the Law of the Sea
WMDs	Weapons of mass destruction

1 Introduction

For States in possession of nuclear weapons, a critical, if not *the* critical, factor in the possession of such weapons is the establishment of a nuclear command, control, and communication (NC3) framework. To put it in rudimentary terms, NC3 is the structure that governs the process that, as its ultimate end product, results in the launch of a nuclear weapon. As Peter Hayes explains:

> NC3 combines wetware (people), hardware (sensor, communications, and control technology), and software (digital code that enables the digital elements to connect people with machines, although much of the technology is analog inherited from a pre-digital era in the older nuclear-armed states). The purpose of this combination is to enable commanders to target, operate, control, and use nuclear weapons by receiving data and advice from sensor systems and people tasked with interpreting it, to make decisions, and to send orders to nuclear forces to move, go on alert, or to strike targets.[1]

NC3 thus governs the entire chain, from when a decision is made to launch a nuclear weapon to the actual launch of that weapon, including any and all advance planning for the use of the weapon, as well as the maintenance of NC3 systems to ensure that the planning and execution are done according to stated doctrine and policy. NC3 systems thus comprise a complex system of people, policy, procedure, infrastructure, and law that governs when, why, how, and by whom the decision to launch a nuclear weapon will be made and executed. As noted by Hayes:

> At a basic and universal level, the NC3 system connects senior nuclear commanders with their nuclear forces and enables them to control their use at all times. Control is a critical concept when it comes to nuclear

1 Peter Hayes, 'Nuclear Command, Control, and Communications (NC3) in Asia-Pacific' (*NAPSNet Special Reports*, 22 September 2021), https://nautilus.org/napsnet/napsnet-special-reports/nuclear-command-control-and-communications-nc3-in-asia-pacific/.

DOI: 10.4324/9781003759294-1

> weapons given their uniquely destructive capability. It is translated by many procedures, measures, and organizational systems. . . . Also integral to NC3 is the notion of legitimacy and authority – the nuclear commander must be accountable under domestic and international law. And there must be systems to ensure that command decisions are authenticated and that nuclear weaponeers know that commands that they receive and act on are authentic and legal.[2]

At its core, NC3 is designed to ensure that a nuclear weapon is *only* launched when sanctioned by proper authorities and that no unsanctioned launch, either intentional or accidental, takes place. To be effective, NC3 systems must therefore fulfil certain critical functions, including detection, warning, and attack characterization; nuclear planning and targeting; decision-making; receiving orders; and enabling the management and direction of forces.[3]

Given the potentially devastating effects of nuclear attack (either sanctioned or unsanctioned), NC3 systems must ensure that any attack is appropriately and correctly characterized as one that gives rise to a right to respond with nuclear force. NC3 systems must also be robust and secure, hardened against any attack that would diminish their ability to fulfil their objectives – they must be strong enough that cyber incursions or similar attacks would not degrade the ability to detect and appropriately characterize incoming attacks.

Furthermore, any response with nuclear force must itself comply with the manifold international laws that govern, inter alia, the use of force and the conduct of hostilities (including the law of targeting, prohibitions on the use of certain weapons, the protection of civilians, and the protection of the natural environment), as well as the law of neutrality and international criminal law. Like any weapons under international law, nuclear weapons, if used, must be used in compliance with it.

All nuclear weapons States have their own unique NC3 systems. However, as explored in this book, there is little uniformity regarding *how* NC3 systems should be established and *how* they should operate. More specifically, there is no set of rules at international law that dictate *how* a nuclear weapons State must structure its NC3 system to ensure that it meets the legal, policy, and security objectives inherent in any NC3 system. Indeed, it is remarkable to note that, given the centrality of NC3 to nuclear doctrine and operations, there is no specific extant reference to NC3 in current international treaty law.

2 Hayes, 'Nuclear Command, Control, and Communications (NC3) in Asia-Pacific'.

3 Adapted from the NC3 of the United States. See further Office of the Deputy Assistant Secretary of Defense for Nuclear Matters, *Nuclear Matters Handbook 2020 [Revised]* (2020), www.acq.osd.mil/ncbdp/nm//NMHB2020rev/.

Moreover, more fundamentally, there appears to be no agreed-upon definition of what NC3 *is* among the nuclear States.[4]

However, the lack of reference to, or definition of, NC3 does not mean that nuclear operations and NC3 are not governed by international law. As surveyed in this book, there is comprehensive law regarding the use of force, the conduct of hostilities, and accountability under international criminal law that is applicable to nuclear weapons operations. In addition, there are numerous nuclear weapons–specific treaties on disarmament, non-proliferation, and nuclear weapon–free zones. However, what is missing from this regulatory landscape is any document or instrument that brings these manifold obligations together in a central source of guidance and instruction.

The fact that, in the 80 years since the first use of nuclear weapons in Hiroshima and Nagasaki, no instrument on NC3 has been adopted might indicate that such an instrument has been unnecessary or superfluous. However, as will be explored in this book, the current legal, political, and security landscape makes it all the more pressing that such a document is adopted. On the political front, nuclear weapons States including Israel, Russia, and the United States have recently been involved in a variety of confrontations, ranging from incidents falling short of war to outright armed conflict in regions such as Ukraine and Eastern Europe, Taiwan and the South China Sea, Gaza and the larger Middle East region, and Venezuela.

On the technical side of things, current NC3 systems find themselves under increasing strain. In some States, existing NC3 hardware is decades old, leaving those States vulnerable to mechanical and operator failure.[5] In addition, emerging threats – such as cyberattacks,[6] AI-driven autonomous weapons, and AI decision-making algorithms[7] – threaten the resilience of

4 In conventional international law practice, the word 'State', when used in reference to a sovereign nation, is capitalized. The current study will follow that practice.

5 For discussion of the issues with legacy NC3 systems, see Peter Hayes, Binoy Kampmark, Philip Reiner, and Deborah Gordon, 'Synthesis Report, NC3 Systems and Strategic Stability: A Global Overview' (*Tech4GS Special Reports*, 6 May 2019), https://securityandtechnology.org/wp-content/uploads/2024/10/nc3_synthesis_report_may_6_2019_IST.pdf.

6 For the potentially devastating impact of cyberattacks against State NC3, see, Michael Ceccarelli, Rachael Harris, Bader Mahmoud, Diego Perez, and Shyla Sharma, 'Impact of Cyberattacks on Functionality of NC3 Systems and Strategic Deterrence' (*Carnegie Mellon University*), https://kilthub.cmu.edu/articles/report/Impact_of_Cyberattacks_on_Functionality_of_NC3_Systems_and_Strategic_Deterrence/21964826; Shane Smith, 'Cyber Threats and Weapons of Mass Destruction', *CSWMD Proceedings* (National Defense University, June 2021), https://inss.ndu.edu/Portals/68/Documents/wmd-proceedings/CSWMD%20Proceedings%20Jun%2021%20PQ.pdf.

7 Regarding AI and NC3, see Anthony Aguirre, Emilia Javorsky, and Max Tegmark, '"Artificial Escalation": Imagining the Future of Nuclear Risk', *Bulletin of the Atomic Scientists* (17 July 2023), https://thebulletin.org/2023/07/artificial-escalation-imagining-the-future-of-nuclear-risk/; Bryce Farabaugh and sdaniels, 'Bad Idea: Integrating Artificial Intelligence with Nuclear Command, Control, and Communications', *Defense360* (3 December 2019), https://defense360.csis.org/bad-idea-integrating-artificial-intelligence-with-nuclear-command-control-and-communications/.

NC3 systems, posing the risk of conflict escalation and, in turn, potentially disrupting effective and accurate communications for nuclear weapons States. The need to clearly outline what rules apply and what best practice should apply, to NC3 is more vital now than ever before.

To that end, this book argues that the international community must adopt an instrument that clearly outlines both the relevant law (the *lex lata*)[8] and the best practice that should be adopted by nuclear weapons States in their establishment and maintenance of nuclear weapons systems. The book argues that a code of conduct governing State NC3 should be created and adopted by States, in order for all States – both nuclear and non-nuclear – to be assured that, in the absence of total and permanent nuclear disarmament, nuclear weapons are only ever used lawfully as a last resort and that any possibility of accidental or incorrect deployment is eradicated.

The book proposes what such a code of conduct should comprise. To understand what best practice in NC3 should look like, the book explores how each nuclear weapons State currently structures its NC3 (if such structures are publicly known) and what international law governs nuclear operations. Additionally, in proposing a model code of conduct, this study will examine the extant literature and practice on the adoption and implementation of non-binding instruments in the international law of armed conflict to better understand how and why non-binding instruments gain traction in State practice. The book will then apply those conclusions to a draft code of conduct for State NC3.

Chapter 2 provides background for the analysis contained in this book. It consists of an (admittedly brief) assessment of the current nuclear landscape and the available information about existing NC3 systems. Chapter 2 will also explore some of the current technical issues that threaten to undermine the integrity of a State's NC3, which inform the underlying thesis of this book. Chapters 3 through 6 then explore the relevant international law that applies to nuclear operations – encompassing, inter alia, international criminal law, the law on the use of force, and the law of armed conflict – in order to set out the legal framework in which NC3 operates. Chapter 7 then examines why a non-binding instrument, such as a code of conduct, would be the preferred model for an NC3 instrument (that is, rather than a binding treaty). Chapter 7 will draw on the wealth of literature on non-binding instruments under international law to explain why they are an emergent and, in some cases, preferred method of international lawmaking and how and why such instruments gain traction and, more importantly, influence in State practice.

8 *Lex lata* is a term in international law meaning 'the law as it exists' – that is, binding international law. It is to be contrasted with *lex ferenda*, or 'future law' – that is, the law that is yet to exist. See Aaron X Fellmeth and Maurice Horwitz, *Guide to Latin in International Law* (Oxford University Press, 2009).

Chapter 8 will then draw on the work of the previous chapters to outline the proposed code of conduct for State NC3 – an instrument comprising 14 rules (divided between *lex lata* and best practice) and a commentary explaining why such rules should exist. Finally, a short conclusion will summarize the findings of this book.

2 The Current Nuclear Landscape

All current declared and undeclared nuclear weapons States maintain their own NC3 systems to manage their nuclear weapon stockpiles. This chapter will explore what is currently known about each nuclear weapons State's stockpiles and anything known about its NC3 infrastructure to discern whether there are any patterns of behaviour, any agreed-upon best practice, and any particular strengths, weaknesses, or vulnerabilities in current NC3 systems.

2.1 Current Nuclear Weapons Inventories

According to the most recent research undertaken by the Stockholm International Peace Research Institute (SIPRI),[1] the worldwide total inventory of nuclear weapons as of January 2026 is as shown in Table 2.1.

As SIPRI notes, all estimates are approximate, updated each year based on new information and revisions of earlier assessments.[2] As indicated by the table, SIPRI was unable to estimate deployment numbers for several nuclear States. While some States (including the United States, the United Kingdom, and France) are relatively transparent regarding their arsenals, others (such as Russia) share information only with other nuclear States (for Russia, this is only with the United States) or disclose little to no information (such as India, Pakistan, and the Democratic People's Republic of Korea [DPRK]).[3]

1 Hans M Kristensen and Matt Korda, 'World Nuclear Forces', in Stockholm International Peace Research Institute (ed), *SIPRI Yearbook 2025: Armaments, Disarmament and International Security* (2025), 14, 15. See also Kristensen and Korda, 'Estimating World Nuclear Forces: An Overview and Assessment of Sources' (*SIPRI*, 14 June 2021).

2 Kristensen and Korda, 'World Nuclear Forces', 178.

3 Kristensen and Korda, 'World Nuclear Forces', 178.

DOI: 10.4324/9781003759294-2

Table 2.1 Nuclear Weapons by State

	Deployed Warheads	*Stored Warheads*	*Total Inventory*
United States	1,770	1,930	3,700
Russia	1,718	2,591	4,309
United Kingdom	120	105	225
France	280	10	290
China	24	576	600
India		180	180
Pakistan		170	170
DPRK		50	50
Israel		90	90
Total	3,912	5,702	9,614

2.2 Current Intelligence on State Nuclear Launch Authorities and Stated Nuclear Doctrine

To understand what might be considered best practice with regard to NC3, it is useful to know what acknowledged (or attributed) State nuclear doctrine is, as well as current known or attributed practice regarding the ultimate authority for nuclear launch.[4]

2.2.1 United States

The US position on nuclear weapons is that, notwithstanding the existence of the Treaty on the Prohibition of Nuclear Weapons (TPNW),[5] there is, for the United States, no customary or treaty prohibition on the possession or use of nuclear weapons in armed conflict.[6] The United States has also not adopted a 'no first use' policy. However, it has stated that it would only use nuclear weapons in extreme circumstances. As noted in the US 2022 *Nuclear Posture Review*:

> As long as nuclear weapons exist, the fundamental role of nuclear weapons is to deter nuclear attack on the United States, our Allies, and partners.

4 This section is not meant to provide more than a general overview. For a more detailed assessment, see Jeffrey G Lewis and Bruno Tertrais, *The Finger on the Button: The Authority to Use Nuclear Weapons in Nuclear-Armed States*, which outlines knowledge regarding each nuclear State's employment authority, procedures for transmission and authentication of launch orders, and devolution procedures – such as what would happen if the person or persons with launch authority were incapacitated. Salma Shaheen's *Nuclear Command and Control Norms: A Comparative Study* (Routledge, 2018) is also a valuable comparative assessment of the command and control regimes of China, India, Pakistan, and the United Kingdom.

5 Treaty on the Prohibition of Nuclear Weapons, opened for signature 20 September 2017, entered into force 22 January 2021, 3379 UNTS 1 (TPNW).

6 US Department of Defense, *Law of War Manual* (June 2015, updated July 2023) (US DoD Law of War Manual), § 6.18.

> The United States would only consider the use of nuclear weapons in extreme circumstances to defend the vital interests of the United States or its Allies and partners.[7]

US nuclear policy outlines that, while the United States considers nuclear weapons to be legal, any use of such weapons is still governed by the law of armed conflict, including:

> Employment of nuclear weapons is subject to the following principles:
>
> 1. The right of the parties to the conflict to adopt means of injuring the enemy is not unlimited.
> 2. It is prohibited to launch attacks against the civilian population as such.
> 3. Distinction must be made at all times between combatants and civilians to the effect the latter be spared as much as possible.
>
> Given their destructive potential, the decision to authorize employment of nuclear weapons should emanate from the highest level of government. For the United States, authority resides solely with the president.[8]

Furthermore, US stated military policy is that the United States 'will not use or threaten to use nuclear weapons against non-nuclear weapons States that are party to the Nuclear Non-Proliferation Treaty and in compliance with their nuclear non-proliferation obligations'.[9]

US nuclear delivery systems are based on the so-called nuclear triad, in which weapons may be delivered from land-based silos (intercontinental ballistic missiles, or ICBMs), by air via strategic bombers, or by nuclear submarines (submarine-launched ballistic missiles, or SLBMs).[10] In the United States, the authority to launch a nuclear weapon resides solely with

7 US Department of Defense, 'Nuclear Posture Review 2022' (2022), 9.

8 US Navy, US Marine Corps, and US Coast Guard, *The Commander's Handbook on The Law of Naval Operations* (NWP 1–14M, MCTP 11–10B, COMDTPUB P5800.7A, March 2022), 10.2.1. Note that the 2022 edition of the *Handbook* still states that there is no treaty prohibition on the use of nuclear weapons in armed conflict, notwithstanding the existence of the TPNW.

9 US DoD Law of War Manual, § 6.18.1. See also US Department of Defense, 'Nuclear Posture Review 2018' (February 2018), 21, US Department of Defense, '2022 National Defense Strategy of the United States of America' (October 2022), 9.
In 2022, France, the United Kingdom, and the United States issued a joint statement, 'P3 Joint Statement on Security Assurances', which stated that negative security assurances *could* include assurances against the use or threat of use of nuclear weapons and reaffirmed the P3's 'existing national security assurances regarding the use or threat of use of nuclear weapons against NNWS Parties to the NPT': see US Department of State, 'P3 Joint Statement on Security Assurances' (4 August 2022), https://2021-2025.state.gov/p3-joint-statement-on-security-assurances/.

10 Darius Watson, 'Rethinking the US Nuclear Triad' (2017) 11 *Strategic Studies Quarterly* 134.

the president. As a practical matter, if US sensors detect an oncoming attack, the president can make a launch decision through, inter alia, the so-called nuclear football – a briefcase containing critical communications equipment and strategic targeting options (from small-scale attacks to all-out bombardment)[11] that is carried by an aide who accompanies the president at all times.

Meanwhile, the president carries the so-called biscuit, a device with a daily-changing code that would be used to authenticate a launch order. Should a nuclear launch be decided upon, the president would contact the National Military Command Centre, read the code on the biscuit, and confirm the chosen target. Once confirmed, the order would be transmitted to US Strategic Command for execution by the relevant launch crew. In all, this process – from order to execution – would take minutes.[12]

The US sole-authority policy is a relic of the Cold War, '*designed* specifically to remove obstacles to a president launching a nuclear attack rather than to create a deliberative process, so that the United States could respond quickly to a Soviet nuclear attack'.[13] Various proposals regarding the introduction of other safeguarding elements into the nuclear decision-making chain of command – including involving the vice president, the Speaker of the House of Representatives, the attorney general, and/or the Supreme Court – have been mooted. However, as of this writing, none have been given serious consideration.[14]

11 See further Alex Wellerstein, 'NC3 Decision Making: Individual Versus Group Process' (*NAPSNet Special Reports*, 8 August 2019), https://nautilus.org/napsnet/napsnet-special-reports/nc3-decision-making-individual-versus-group-process/.

12 Eryn MacDonald, 'Whose Finger Is on the Button? Nuclear Launch Authority in the United States and Other Nations' (*Issue Brief*, Union of Concerned Scientists, 2017). See also David S Jonas and Bryn McWhorter, 'Nuclear Launch Authority: Too Big a Decision for Just the President' (*Arms Control Association*, June 2021).
As Boothby and Heintschel von Heinegg note in *The Law on Nuclear Weapons: An International Commentary* (p. 296), '[I]t is interesting and highly significant – for example, in relation to the question of potential criminal liability – that the US DoD Law of War Manual specifies that the authority to launch is governmental in nature and, accordingly, is not a matter for an individual military commander'.

13 MacDonald, 'Whose Finger Is on the Button?', 1. See also Jonas and McWhorter, 'Nuclear Launch Authority'; Scott D Sagan and Allen S Weiner, 'The Rule of Law and the Role of Strategy in U.S. Nuclear Doctrine' (2021) 45 *International Security* 126; Jeffrey G Lewis and Scott D Sagan, 'The Nuclear Necessity Principle: Making U.S. Targeting Policy Conform with Ethics & the Laws of War' (2016) 145 *Dædalus: Journal of the American Academy of Arts & Sciences* 62.

14 See Lisbeth Gronlund, David Wright, and Steve Fetter, 'An Expert Proposal: How to Limit Presidential Authority to Order the Use of Nuclear Weapons', *Bulletin of the Atomic Scientists* (8 January 2021), https://thebulletin.org/2021/01/an-expert-proposal-how-to-limit-presidential-authority-to-order-the-use-of-nuclear-weapons/.

The NC3 of the United States[15] is undergoing a process of updating,[16] including separating some conventional and nuclear infrastructure,[17] but is still largely a mix of legacy Cold War systems and more modern technologies, including:

- launch detection satellites in geosynchronous and other orbits that, within minutes after launch, detect the hot infrared signal generated during boost;
- large, ground-based, phased-array early warning radars that detect launches in mid-course (10–20 minutes after launch) and provide independent confirmation of attack;
- facilities located in Colorado Springs and elsewhere to interpret early warning information and assess the nature and scope of the attack;
- air, ground-mobile, and fixed command centres that, among other things, provide venues to establish a conference to advise the president; and
- survivable communications links that transmit raw early warning data to users, provide secure means to advise the president from afar, and convey execution messages to force elements, as well as messages to cease hostilities.[18]

2.2.2 Russia

The most recent information regarding launch authority and nuclear doctrine in Russia is contained in the 2024 publication 'Fundamentals of State Policy of the Russian Federation on Nuclear Deterrence'. That document notes that launch authority resides with the Russian president and states:

> 19. The conditions that enable the possibility of nuclear weapons employment by the Russian Federation are as follows:
>
> a) receipt of reliable data on the launch of ballistic missiles attacking the territories of the Russian Federation and (or) its allies;
> b) employment of nuclear or other types of weapons of mass destruction by an adversary against the territories of the Russian Federation and

15 See generally James J Wirtz and Jeffrey A Larsen (eds), *Nuclear Command, Control, and Communications: A Primer on US Systems and Future Challenges* (Georgetown University Press, 2022).

16 See further Kristensen and Korda, 'World Nuclear Forces', 179; Hans M Kristensen, Matt Korda, Eliana Johns, and Mackenzie Knight, 'United States Nuclear Weapons, 2025' (2025) 81 *Bulletin of the Atomic Scientists* 53.

17 See, for example, Robert Samuel Wilson and Russell Rumbaugh, 'Reversal of Nuclear-Conventional Entanglement in Outer Space' (2024) 47 *Journal of Strategic Studies* 64.

18 John R Harvey, 'U.S. Nuclear Command and Control for the 21st Century' (*NAPSNet Special Reports*, 24 May 2019), https://nautilus.org/napsnet/napsnet-special-reports/u-s-nuclear-command-and-control-for-the-21st-century/.

(or) its allies, against facilities and (or) military formations of the Russian Federation located outside its territory;

c) actions by an adversary affecting elements of critically important state or military infrastructure of the Russian Federation, the disablement of which would disrupt response actions by nuclear forces;
d) aggression against the Russian Federation and (or) the Republic of Belarus as participants in the Union State with the employment of conventional weapons, which creates a critical threat to their sovereignty and (or) territorial integrity;
e) receipt of reliable data on the massive launch (take-off) of air and space attack means (strategic and tactical aircraft, cruise missiles, unmanned, hypersonic and other aerial vehicles) and their crossing of the state border of the Russian Federation.[19]

Regarding its NC3, Russia maintains a system, known as 'the Cheget' – a system of three briefcases linking the Russian president to the Russian NC3 system. It transmits launch orders to the central Russian military command. From there, the central command accesses the launch codes, which are then transmitted to the individual weapons commanders, who initiate launch procedures. A backup system, known as Perimetr, allows the central command to bypass the individual commanders and directly initiate the launch of land-based missiles.[20] Currently, it is not definitively known whether all three briefcases are required in order to initiate a launch, though there is some evidence to indicate that the command code must be received from at least two terminals.[21] Russian nuclear weapons delivery systems are, like those of the United States, based on the nuclear triad.[22] And, like the United States, Russia is engaged in a process of modernization of its nuclear forces.[23]

2.2.3 United Kingdom

The United Kingdom's Integrated Review Refresh 2023 reaffirmed its stated nuclear policy and launch authority – that the United Kingdom would

19 Ministry of Foreign Affairs of the Russian Federation, 'Fundamentals of State Policy of the Russian Federation on Nuclear Deterrence' (19 November 2024), www.mid.ru/en/foreign_policy/international_safety/1434131/. See also Hans M Kristensen, Matt Korda, Eliana Johns, and Mackenzie Knight, 'Russian Nuclear Weapons, 2025' (2025) 81 *Bulletin of the Atomic Scientists* 208.

20 Reuters, 'The Chain of Command for Potential Russian Nuclear Strikes', *Reuters* (3 March 2022), www.reuters.com/world/europe/what-is-chain-command-potential-russian-nuclear-strikes-2022-03-02/.

21 Leonid Ryabikhin, 'Russia's NC3 and Early Warning Systems' (*NAPSNet Special Reports*, 11 July 2019), https://nautilus.org/napsnet/napsnet-special-reports/russias-nc3-and-early-warning-systems/.

22 See Kristensen et al, 'Russian Nuclear Weapons, 2025'.

23 See further Kristensen and Korda, 'World Nuclear Forces', 179.

'consider using our nuclear weapons only in extreme circumstances of self-defence, including the defence of our NATO allies. Only the Prime Minister can authorize their use'.[24] Furthermore, as outlined in the UK *Manual of the Law of Armed Conflict*, 'The threshold for the legitimate use of nuclear weapons is clearly a high one' and 'The United Kingdom would only consider using nuclear weapons in self-defence, including the defence of its NATO allies, and even then only in extreme circumstances'.[25]

The *Manual of the Law of Armed Conflict* states,

> There is no specific rule of international law, express or implied, which prohibits the use of nuclear weapons. The legality of their use depends upon the application of the general rules of international law, including those regulating the use of force and the conduct of hostilities.[26]

Likewise, the *Manual* notes that the UK has given a unilateral assurance not to threaten to use nuclear weapons against States party to the Treaty on the Non-Proliferation of Nuclear Weapons (NPT).[27] In giving that assurance, the United Kingdom has emphasized 'the need for universal adherence to and compliance with the NPT' and noted that 'this assurance would not apply to any state in material breach of those non-proliferation obligations'.[28] UK stated doctrine also notes that the United Kingdom reserves the right to right to 'review this assurance if the future threat of weapons of mass destruction, such as chemical and biological capabilities, or emerging technologies that could have a comparable impact, makes it necessary'.[29]

Regarding NC3, the United Kingdom's nuclear weapons are located on four ballistic missile submarines (SSBNs), which are involved in part of a continuous at-sea deterrence system[30] known as Operation Relentless. At

24 UK Government, 'Integrated Review Refresh 2023: Responding to a More Contested and Volatile World' (March 2023), 33.

25 UK Ministry of Defence, *The Joint Service Manual of the Law of Armed Conflict* (JSP 383, 2004) (UK LOAC Manual), para 6.17.1.

26 UK LOAC Manual, para 6.17 (footnotes omitted). The Manual was published prior to the entry into force of the TPNW.

27 Treaty on the Non-Proliferation of Nuclear Weapons, 1 July 1968, entered into force 5 March 1970, 729 UNTS 161 (NPT).

28 UK Government, *Securing Britain in an Age of Uncertainty: The Strategic Defence and Security Review* (HM Government, October 2010), para 3.7.

29 UK Government, 'Integrated Review of Security, Defence, Development and Foreign Policy 2021: Nuclear Deterrent' (17 March 2021), www.gov.uk/guidance/integrated-review-of-security-defence-development-and-foreign-policy-2021-nuclear-deterrent.

30 Hans M Kristensen, Matt Korda, Eliana Johns, and Mackenzie Knight, 'United Kingdom Nuclear Weapons, 2024' (2024) 80 *Bulletin of the Atomic Scientists* 394; Hans M Kristensen, Matt Korda, Eliana Johns, and Mackenzie Knight, 'The Changing Nuclear Landscape in Europe' (2025) 81 *Bulletin of the Atomic Scientists* 485.

any given time, one of the four SSBNs is operationally active,[31] with the remainder located at HM Naval Base Clyde.[32] Should the decision be made to launch, the UK Prime Minister will communicate the order to the Ministry of Defence from a secure location capable of communicating the order to the SSBN:

> The message is authenticated . . . and encoded, and from the moment it leaves the PM's hand it is handled at all stages by two nuclear-authenticated operators following strict protocols. The order is transmitted to the patrolling SSBN through several communication paths appropriate to the crisis; at least one of these can survive even a devastating nuclear attack upon the UK. On arrival onboard the SSBN, the message is authenticated by two officers (neither of whom is the Commanding Officer) and decoded using two separate cryptography sets (and matching the two sets of cryptography used by the original officers in the presence of the PM) and the submarine follows the instructions regarding the targeting of the missiles and ordered launch time, manoeuvring to remain undetected and secure to a position from which it can conduct the launch unmolested and undetected until the directed launch time.[33]

2.2.4 France

France's stated nuclear policy is that it must 'maintain a robust and credible nuclear deterrent to prevent a major war, guarantee France's freedom of action and defend its vital interests, which have a European dimension'.[34] This policy must be read in line with statements in France's 2012 *Manuel de droit des conflits armés*[35] that, while nuclear weapons are not specifically and absolutely prohibited by international law, they are nonetheless subject to the law of armed conflict, which limits methods and means of combat, prohibiting

31 UK Defence Nuclear Organisation and Ministry of Defence, 'UK's Nuclear Deterrent (CASD)' (16 March 2021), www.gov.uk/government/collections/uks-nuclear-deterrent-casd. See also UK Defence Nuclear Organisation and Ministry of Defence, 'Dreadnought Submarine Programme: Factsheet' (16 March 2021), www.gov.uk/government/publications/successor-submarine-programme-factsheet/successor-submarine-programme-factsheet.

32 Royal Navy, 'HMNB Clyde', www.royalnavy.mod.uk/our-organisation/bases-and-stations/naval-base/clyde.

33 John Gower, 'United Kingdom: Nuclear Weapon Command, Control, and Communications: Technology for Global Security Special Report' (*Tech4GS Special Reports*, 15 August 2019), 8–9.

34 République Française, 'National Strategic Review 2022' (November 2022), 33, www.sgdsn.gouv.fr/files/files/rns-uk-20221202.pdf.

35 French Ministère de la Défense, 'Manuel de droit des conflits armés' (2012), 22 https://defenseetsecuriteinternationale.files.wordpress.com/2013/10/manuel_de_droit_des_conflits_armes.pdf.

weapons of a nature to have indiscriminate effects and those that cause superfluous injury or unnecessary suffering.[36]

Research[37] indicates that decisions to use nuclear weapons would generally involve only three people: the president, the chief of the presidential military staff, and the chief of the defence staff,[38] though the latter two persons serve in an advisory capacity only, with the ultimate decision to launch resting with the president.[39] In terms of French NC3, there is little information that is publicly available. Current research suggests that any order to launch, once decided upon, would emanate either from the Elysée Palace or from the mobile command post – the *PC léger déplaçable*. From there, the order would go to the chair of the joint chiefs of staff, where it would be transmitted to either French SSBNs or French aircraft and verified by specialists.[40] Any launch decision is subject to the two-person rule.[41]

2.2.5 China

China's stated nuclear doctrine has been reiterated in documents submitted to the United Nations regarding its compliance with the NPT,[42] in which it reiterates its defensive nuclear strategy[43] and its clear commitment not to use nuclear weapons against non-nuclear weapons States or nuclear weapon–free zones.[44]

36 Note that a similar statement was *not* included in French Ministère des Armées, 'Manuel de droit des opérations militaires' (2022). However, that manual affirmed the general principles of the law of armed conflict as including limits on the methods and means of combat, and prohibitions on weapons of a nature to have indiscriminate effects and those that cause superfluous injury or unnecessary suffering: at 109.

37 Benoît Pelopidas, 'France: Nuclear Command, Control, and Communications' (*NAPSNet Special Reports*, 10 June 2019), https://nautilus.org/napsnet/napsnet-special-reports/france-nuclear-command-control-and-communications/. See also Hans M Kristensen, Matt Korda, Eliana Johns, and Mackenzie Knight, 'French Nuclear Weapons, 2025' (2025) 81 *Bulletin of the Atomic Scientists* 313.

38 See Lewis and Tertrais, *The Finger on the Button*, 16–19.

39 Lewis and Tertrais, *The Finger on the Button*, 16.

40 See also Kristensen et al, 'French Nuclear Weapons, 2025'.

41 Pelopidas, 'France: Nuclear Command, Control, and Communications'.

42 For the Chinese national doctrine, see China, *Implementation of the Treaty on the Non-Proliferation of Nuclear Weapons in the People's Republic of China: Report Submitted by China*, 2020 Review Conference of the Parties to the Treaty on the Non-Proliferation of Nuclear Weapons, UN Doc NPT/CONF.2020/41 (16 November 2021).

43 See State Council Information Office of the People's Republic of China, 'China's National Defense in the New Era' (July 2019), https://english.www.gov.cn/archive/whitepaper/201907/24/content_WS5d3941ddc6d08408f502283d.html.

44 China, *Implementation of the Treaty on the Non-Proliferation of Nuclear Weapons in the People's Republic of China: Report Submitted by China*, Preparatory Committee for the 2020 Review Conference of the Parties to the Treaty on the Non-Proliferation of Nuclear Weapons, UN Doc NPT/CONF.2020/PC.III/8 (29 April 2019), paras 7, 71.

Current research indicates that the ultimate authority to launch nuclear weapons resides with the Standing Committee of the Politburo of the Central Committee, which includes China's top military leaders on the Central Military Commission and the top political leaders on the Politburo.[45] In regard to China's policy on the use of nuclear weapons, the Ministry of National Defence of the People's Republic of China states:

> China is always committed to a nuclear policy of no first use of nuclear weapons at any time and under any circumstances, and not using or threatening to use nuclear weapons against non-nuclear-weapon states or nuclear-weapon-free zones unconditionally. China advocates the ultimate complete prohibition and thorough destruction of nuclear weapons. China does not engage in any nuclear arms race with any other country and keeps its nuclear capabilities at the minimum level required for national security. China pursues a nuclear strategy of self-defense, the goal of which is to maintain national strategic security by deterring other countries from using or threatening to use nuclear weapons against China.[46]

China's NC3 regulates a primarily land-based missile system, though recent research suggests that China is expanding into sea- and air-based systems.[47] Research also indicates that Chinese nuclear and non-nuclear arsenals share a command-and-control system,[48] though missiles and warheads are separated when forces are at peacetime alert status.[49] The most recent assessment of China's nuclear arsenal has found, inter alia, that China is rapidly expanding and modernizing its nuclear arsenal,[50] including its dual-capable

45 Fiona S Cunningham, 'Nuclear Command, Control, and Communications Systems of the People's Republic of China' (*NAPSNet Special Reports*, 18 July 2019), https://nautilus.org/napsnet/napsnet-special-reports/nuclear-command-control-and-communications-systems-of-the-peoples-republic-of-china/, citing Jiang Tiejun, *Dang de Guofang He Jundui Gaige Sixiang Yanjiu [Research on Party Defense and Military Reform Thought]* (Junshi Kexue Yuan Chubanshe, 2015), 79.

46 State Council Information Office of the People's Republic of China, *China's National Defense in the New Era*.

47 Hans M Kristensen, Matt Korda, Eliana Johns, and Mackenzie Knight, 'Chinese Nuclear Weapons, 2025' (2025) 81 *Bulletin of the Atomic Scientists* 135.

48 Ariel E Levite, Lyu Jinghua, George Perkovich, Lu Chuanying, Xu Manshu, Li Bin, and Yang Fan, 'China-U.S. Cyber-Nuclear C3 Stability' (*Carnegie Endowment for International Peace*, April 2021), https://carnegieendowment.org/research/2021/04/china-us-cyber-nuclear-c3-stability. See also Peter Hayes, 'Nuclear Command, Control, and Communications (NC3) in Asia-Pacific' (*NAPSNet Special Reports*, 22 September 2021), https://nautilus.org/napsnet/napsnet-special-reports/nuclear-command-control-and-communications-nc3-in-asia-pacific/.

49 Cunningham, 'Nuclear Command, Control, and Communications Systems of the People's Republic of China'.

50 Kristensen et al, 'Chinese Nuclear Weapons, 2025'.

intermediate-range ballistic missile (IRBM)[51] force, and is refitting its SSBNs with longer-range submarine-launched ballistic missiles. China has also reassigned an operational nuclear mission to its bombers, with the aim of developing an air-launched ballistic missile (ALBM) that might have nuclear capability.[52]

Any launch that was ordered by the Central Military Commission would likely be transmitted to the Joint Operations Command Centre and from there to Rocket Force Headquarters, to missile bases, and then to launch platforms and crew.[53] Intelligence indicates that China is likely developing a space-based early warning system, which would allow it to 'shift to a launch-under-attack alert status if it chose to do so in the future. A Chinese space-based early warning system is, however, unlikely to be operational for approximately another decade'.[54]

2.2.6 India

Research indicates that India maintains a 'no first use' policy[55] and that, as stated in 2003, India would not use nuclear weapons against States that do not possess such capability, although it reserves the right to use nuclear weapons in response to any attack employing weapons of mass destruction (WMDs), including biological or chemical weapons.[56] India has publicly stated that it will not become party to the TPNW, and it 'shall not be bound by any of the obligations that may arise from it', expressing the view that the treaty 'does not constitute or contribute to the development of customary international law'.[57]

51 A dual-capable missile is one capable of being deployed with both conventional and nuclear warheads. What this means is that a strike order monitored on a communications system might pertain to a nuclear or conventional warhead, and a missile observed to be readying for use may be nuclear or conventionally armed. The use of dual-capable missiles obviously makes it ambiguous for observers as to whether a nuclear strike has been ordered. See further PW Singer and Ma Xiu, 'China's Ambiguous Missile Strategy Is Risky', *Popular Science* (11 May 2020), www.popsci.com/story/blog-network/eastern-arsenal/china-nuclear-conventional-missiles/.

52 Kristensen et al, 'Chinese Nuclear Weapons, 2025'.

53 Hayes, 'Nuclear Command, Control, and Communications (NC3) in Asia-Pacific'.

54 Cunningham, 'Nuclear Command, Control, and Communications Systems of the People's Republic of China'.

55 Kumar Sundaram and MV Ramana, 'India and the Policy of No First Use of Nuclear Weapons' (2018) 1 *Journal for Peace and Nuclear Disarmament* 152.

56 See Toby Dalton, 'Much Ado about India's No-First-Use Nuke Policy' (*Carnegie Endowment for International Peace*, 26 September 2019) (originally published in *India Global Business*, September 2019), https://carnegieendowment.org/2019/09/26/much-ado-about-india-s-no-first-use-nuke-policy-pub-79952. See also Sundaram and Ramana, 'India and the Policy of No First Use of Nuclear Weapons'.

57 Indian Ministry of External Affairs, 'India's View on the Treaty on the Prohibition of Nuclear Weapons' (*Press Release*, 22 January 2021), www.mea.gov.in/press-releases.htm?dtl/33409/Indias+view+on+the+Treaty+on+the+Prohibition+of+Nuclear+Weapons.

Launch authority for nuclear weapons in India rests with the Nuclear Command Authority,[58] established in 2003,[59] which comprises a political council, chaired by the prime minister, and an executive council, chaired by the national security adviser to the prime minister.[60] Although there is little in the way of official published doctrine, it is 'widely understood that the prime minister likely holds the employment authority'.[61] Beyond this, little is publicly known regarding Indian NC3. Current literature suggests that India has pursued an NC3 structure that is designed to survive a first strike and is hardened against radiation or electronic interference and disruption, with numerous redundancies built into the system to strengthen survivability. The Nuclear Command Authority is believed to work off a two-person rule for access to and delivery of nuclear weapons, with a nuclear triad of air-, land-, and sea-based delivery systems.[62]

2.2.7 Pakistan

Like India, Pakistan has pledged a position of 'no first use' against non-nuclear weapons States but has retained the right to first use of nuclear weapons against a nuclear armed aggressor and that it would use nuclear weapons for defensive purposes in any armed conflict with India.[63] Pakistan's policy is one of 'full-spectrum deterrence':[64] Pakistan must possess a 'full spectrum of nuclear weapons in three categories: strategic, operational and tactical, with full range coverage of the large Indian land mass and its outlying territories', with the aim that 'there is no place for India's strategic weapons to hide' and to ensure deterrence of 'the adversary's declared policy of massive retaliation'.[65]

58 In some research, this is referred to as the National Command Authority; Lewis and Tertrais, *The Finger on the Button*, 24.

59 See further Lewis and Tertrais, *The Finger on the Button*, 24; Lauren J Borja and MV Ramana, 'Command and Control of India's Nuclear Arsenal' (2020) 3 *Journal for Peace and Nuclear Disarmament* 1.

60 Lewis and Tertrais, *The Finger on the Button*. See also Harsh V Pant, 'India's Nuclear Doctrine and Command Structure: Implications for India and the World' (2005) 24 *Comparative Strategy* 277.

61 Lewis and Tertrais, *The Finger on the Button*, 24. See also Rajat Pandit, 'Narendra Modi Has His Finger Now on India's Nuclear Button', *Times of India* (27 May 2014), http://timesofindia.indiatimes.com/news/Narendra-Modi-has-his-finger-now-on-Indias-nuclearbutton/articleshow/35625045.cms.

62 See generally Sanjana Gogna, 'The Nasr and India's Nuclear Command Structure, Strategy and Doctrine' (2023) 42 *Comparative Strategy* 50; Hans M Kristensen, Matt Korda, Eliana Johns, and Mackenzie Knight, 'Indian Nuclear Weapons, 2024' (2024) 80 *Bulletin of the Atomic Scientists* 326.

63 See Claire Mills, 'Nuclear Weapons at a Glance: India and Pakistan' (*Research Briefing*, House of Commons Library, 29 July 2022), 15, https://researchbriefings.files.parliament.uk/documents/CBP-9070/CBP-9070.pdf; Alicia Sanders-Zakre and Kelsey Davenport, 'Is India Shifting Nuclear Doctrine?', *Arms Control Today* (May 2017), www.armscontrol.org/act/2017-05/news/india-shifting-nuclear-doctrine.

64 Khalid Kidwai, '25 Years of Yom Takbeer: Promoting Peace, Stability and Development' (*Speech*, Arms Control and Disarmament Centre/Institute of Strategic Studies Islamabad, 24 May 2023), https://issi.org.pk/speech-by-lt-gen-retd-khalid-kidwai-advisor-national-command-authority-and-former-dg-spd-on-25th-youme-e-takbeer/.

65 Khalid Kidwai, '25 Years of Yom Takbeer'.

Pakistan's nuclear authority rests with the National Command Authority (NCA). Established in 2000 and originally chaired by the president, the NCA has been chaired by the prime minister since 2009 (following the National Command Authority Act of 2010).[66] The NCA is made up of two committees – the Employment Control Committee and the Development Control Committee – the membership of which includes civilian and military officials, such as the chair of the joint chiefs of staff, the Minister of Defence, the Minister of Foreign Affairs, the commanders of each branch of the armed forces, and the Director-General of the Strategic Planning Division (though, reportedly, any person in this role no longer sits as a full ex officio member). Any decision to use nuclear weapons would require a decision (preferably unanimous but, at a minimum, by majority) by the NCA, with the chair casting the final vote.[67]

Research suggests that Pakistan's NC3 is based on space- and land-based communications systems with in-built redundancy, controlling land-based and air delivery systems.[68] Research also suggests that the system is vulnerable to 'disruption, counter-measures, and physical attack'.[69] Moreover, Pakistan's early-warning systems, in the form of satellites and radar detection, have apparently limited range and are likewise systemically fragile, with Pakistan being largely dependent on US and Chinese strategic satellite support and air defence radars that are capable of providing only limited warning of incoming air- or missile-based attacks.[70]

2.2.8 Democratic People's Republic of Korea

The stated nuclear policy of the DPRK is found in a 2013 law, revised in 2022 and then enshrined in a 2023 constitutional amendment,[71] which proclaims:

> The DPRK shall regard it as its main principle to use nuclear weapons as the last means in order to cope with outside aggression and attack seriously threatening the security of the country and the people.

66 As noted in Lewis and Tertrais, *The Finger on the Button*, 27; Feroz Hassan Khan, 'Nuclear Command, Control and Communications (NC3): The Case of Pakistan' (*NAPSNet Special Reports*, 26 September 2019), https://nautilus.org/napsnet/napsnet-special-reports/nuclear-command-control-and-communications-nc3-the-case-of-pakistan/.

67 Khan, 'Nuclear Command, Control and Communications (NC3): The Case of Pakistan'.

68 Tahir Mahmood Azad and Karl Dewey, 'Assessing the Security of Pakistan's Nuclear Weapon Programme' (2023) 39 *Defense & Security Analysis* 123, 128. See also Hans M Kristensen, Matt Korda, Eliana Johns, and Mackenzie Knight, 'Pakistan Nuclear Weapons, 2025' (2025) 81 *Bulletin of the Atomic Scientists* 386.

69 Khan, 'Nuclear Command, Control and Communications (NC3): The Case of Pakistan'.

70 Hayes, 'Nuclear Command, Control, and Communications (NC3) in Asia-Pacific'.

71 Soo-Hyang Choi and Hyonhee Shin, 'North Korea Amends Constitution on Nuclear Policy, Cites US Provocations', *Reuters* (28 September 2023), www.reuters.com/world/asia-pacific/north-korea-parliament-amends-constitution-enshrine-nuclear-policy-kcna-2023-09-27/.

> The DPRK shall neither threaten non-nuclear weapons states with its nuclear weapons nor use nuclear weapons against them unless they join aggression or attack against the DPRK in collusion with other nuclear weapons states.[72]

However, the DPRK does not appear to affirm a 'no first use' principle, with the law going on to state the circumstances in which nuclear weapons would be used as including:

> In case an attack by nuclear weapons or other weapons of mass destruction was launched or drew near is judged
>
> In case a nuclear or non-nuclear attack by hostile forces on the state leadership and the command organization of the state's nuclear forces was launched or drew near is judged
>
> In case a fatal military attack against important strategic objects of the state was launched or drew near is judged
>
> In case the need for operation for preventing the expansion and protraction of a war and taking the initiative in the war in contingency is inevitably raised.
>
> In other case an inevitable situation in which it is compelled to correspond with catastrophic crisis to the existence of the state and safety of the people by only nuclear weapons is created.[73]

The DPRK's nuclear authorization protocol provides that nuclear weapons 'can be used only by a final order of the Supreme Commander of the Korean People's Army (KPA)', which, since 2016, is a position held by the chairman of the State Affairs Commission – currently Kim Jong-Un.[74] Therefore, any decision to launch would rest with Kim Jong-Un alone. Beyond this, very little is known regarding the structure (or even existence) of the DPRK's NC3

72 KCNA Watch, 'Law on DPRK's Policy on Nuclear Forces Promulgated', *Korean Central News Agency* (9 September 2022), https://kcnawatch.org/newstream/1662687258-950776986/law-on-dprks-policy-on-nuclear-forces-promulgated/.

73 KCNA Watch, 'Law on DPRK's Policy on Nuclear Forces Promulgated'. See also Bruce Klingner, 'The Troubling New Changes to North Korea's Nuclear Doctrine' (*Backgrounder* [The Heritage Foundation], No 3729, 17 October 2022), www.heritage.org/asia/report/the-troubling-new-changes-north-koreas-nuclear-doctrine; Wook-Sik Cheong, 'The DPRK's Changed Nuclear Doctrine: Factors and Implications' (2023) 6 *Journal for Peace and Nuclear Disarmament* 136; Edward Kwon, 'North Korea's Nuclear Strategy and the Direction of WMD Development' (2020) 33 *Journal of East Asian Affairs* 276.

74 'Law on Consolidating Position of Nuclear Weapons State Adopted', *Korean Central News Agency* (1 April 2013), as cited in Lewis and Tertrais, *The Finger on the Button*, 30. See also Myeongguk Cheon, 'DPRK'S NC3 System' (*NAPSNet Special Reports*, 6 June 2019), https://nautilus.org/napsnet/napsnet-special-reports/dprks-nc3-system/.

system:[75] Delivery systems are based on intercontinental ballistic missiles and submarine-launched ballistic missiles, but there are weaknesses in the systems, not least of which is that the DPRK currently lacks long-range early warning systems.[76]

2.2.9 Israel

Israel pursues a policy of *amimut* or 'nuclear opacity and ambiguity'.[77] It neither confirms nor denies its possession of nuclear weapons and has not carried out any nuclear tests.[78] The only official statements have repeated the position that 'Israel will not be the first country to introduce nuclear weapons in the Middle East'.[79] Due to scarce information regarding the Israeli nuclear program, it is difficult to say what Israel's nuclear doctrine is or who retains the ultimate authority to launch nuclear weapons. However, as noted by Israeli nuclear weapons expert Avner Cohen, it is likely that the Israeli launch authority is shared by, at a minimum, the prime minister and the Minister of Defence so that no single person can authorize a launch.[80] Recent research seems to confirm this appraisal: 'In Israel, leaders are unable to use nuclear weapons unilaterally and are constitutionally forced to deliberate with other senior establishment figures before nuclear use'.[81]

75 Ildo Hwang, 'North Korea's Nuclear Command and Control Estimate: Variables and Trends' (2021) 33 *Korean Journal of Defense Analysis* 617, 629. See also Shane Smith and Paul Berstein, 'North Korean Nuclear Command and Control: Alternatives and Implications' (*Strategic Trends Research Initiative, Defence Threat Reduction Agency*, August 2022), https://wmdcenter.ndu.edu/Portals/97/Documents/Publications/NK-Nuclear-Command-and-Control_Report.pdf.

76 Hayes, 'Nuclear Command, Control, and Communications (NC3) in Asia-Pacific'. See also Cheon, 'DPRK'S NC3 System'; Hans M Kristensen, Matt Korda, Eliana Johns, and Mackenzie Knight, 'North Korean Nuclear Weapons, 2024' (2024) 80 *Bulletin of the Atomic Scientists* 251.

77 Ofer Israeli, 'Israel's Nuclear Amimut Policy and Its Consequences' (2015) 21 *Israel Affairs* 541.

78 Claire Mills, 'Nuclear Weapons Profile: Israel' (*Research Briefing*, House of Commons Library, 29 July 2022), https://researchbriefings.files.parliament.uk/documents/CBP-9075/CBP-9075.pdf. See also Avner Cohen, 'Israel's NC3 Profile: Opaque Nuclear Governance' (*NAPSNet Special Reports*, 11 October 2019), https://nautilus.org/napsnet/napsnet-special-reports/israels-nc3-profile-opaque-nuclear-governance/.

79 Information Memorandum from the President's Special Assistant (Rostow) to President Johnson, 12 December 1968, reprinted in *Foreign Relations of the United States, 1964–1968, Volume XX: Arab-Israeli Dispute, 1967–68*, https://history.state.gov/historicaldocuments/frus1964-68v20/d349.

80 See Avner Cohen, *The Worst-Kept Secret: Israel's Bargain with the Bomb* (Columbia University Press, 2010), 97, seemingly confirmed by a podcast interview with Ehud Barak: Lior Kodner, 'Podcast Interview with Ehud Barak', *Haaretz* (26 March 2019), www.haaretz.co.il/digital/podcast/.premium-1.7059848.

81 Sebastian Brixey-Williams and Paul Ingram, 'Responsible Nuclear Sovereignty and the Future of the Global Nuclear Order' (*BASIC and the University of Birmingham's Institute for Conflict, Cooperation and Security*, 2017), 6, https://basicint.org/wp-content/uploads/2018/06/Brixey-Williams-and-Ingram-Responsible-Nuclear-Sovereignty-Report-PDF_FINAL-2017.pdf.

In terms of what is known of Israel's specific NC3 system, as Cohen notes, 'Under Israel's policy of nuclear opacity there is virtually no open and authorized information on the country's nuclear governance and its related NC3 architecture'.[82] Studies of the Israeli nuclear program indicate that the fundamental superstructure of current Israeli NC3 includes the following provisions:

- The Israel Defense Forces (IDF) remain a conventional army in their basic orientation (both force structure and doctrine), as long as Israel faces conventional threats.
- The nuclear program should be viewed as a national security insurance policy under the control of the prime minister, not as another military system under the custodianship of the IDF.
- Israel remains politically committed to not introducing nuclear weapons to the Middle East.[83]
- The utility of the nuclear weapons is mostly political, not military.
- The nuclear issue should be handled with extreme caution and care by its political and professional custodians and by all civilians, and it must not be a vehicle to change how the IDF operates as a conventionally armed military.
- Because its nuclear weapons program requires extraordinary secrecy and because democratic procedures may be bypassed, national consensus is essential.[84]

According to best current understanding, Israel continues to maintain a strict physical and organizational separation between nuclear and conventional assets: Current research suggests that Israeli nuclear delivery platforms include land-based ballistic missiles and nuclear-capable aircraft,[85] with a sea-based second-strike capability.[86] Beyond this, little is known in open-source literature about the details of Israeli NC3.

82 Cohen, 'Israel's NC3 Profile'.

83 Note that Israel has 'resisted several international calls for a Middle East WMD Free Zone in the Middle East', taking the position that States in the Middle East must recognize the State of Israel and establish peaceful relations with Israel before negotiations for a nuclear weapon–free zone can begin. See further Wael Al Assad, 'The Quest for a WMD Free Zone in the Middle East: History, Lessons Learned, and the Way Forward' (2022) 5 *Journal for Peace and Nuclear Disarmament* 114, 116; Nuclear Threat Initiative, 'Nuclear Disarmament Israel' (*Fact Sheet*, 15 November 2023), www.nti.org/analysis/articles/israel-nuclear-disarmament/.

84 Cohen, *The Worst-Kept Secret*, 62–67.

85 Hans M Kristensen and Matt Korda, 'Israeli Nuclear Weapons 2021' (2022) 78 *Bulletin of the Atomic Scientists* 38, 44–47.

86 Cohen, 'Israel's NC3 Profile'. See also Rubina Waseem, 'Flux in the Middle East and Nuclear Israel' (2020) 6 *Journal of Security and Strategic Analyses* 55, 66–68.

2.2.10 Other Nuclear Umbrella States

Finally, it should be noted that any consideration of nuclear weapons usage and NC3 must also consider 'nuclear umbrella'[87] arrangements and other security arrangements regarding nuclear weapons. These arrangements would include:

- NATO, which in its 2022 Strategic Concept,[88] emphasized that 'as long as nuclear weapons exist, NATO will remain a nuclear alliance', but it will also 'seek to create the security environment for a world without nuclear weapons'.[89] Accordingly, 'NATO's deterrence and defence posture' will continue to be 'based on an appropriate mix of nuclear, conventional and missile defence capabilities, complemented by space and cyber capabilities'.[90] The Strategic Concept emphasizes that 'the circumstances in which NATO might have to use nuclear weapons are extremely remote'.[91] Of the NATO States, five are NATO nuclear delivery States: Belgium, Germany, Italy, the Netherlands, and Türkiye, each of which maintains its own NC3 system[92] that would be activated after wartime transfer by the United States of nuclear weapons for delivery on its bombers.[93] The remaining NATO States rely on the United States via NATO for extended nuclear deterrence.
- ANZUS – the security alliance between Australia, New Zealand, and the United States.[94] While the text of ANZUS does not mention nuclear weapons, it is, nonetheless, a security alliance treaty and is treated, in practice,

87 'Nuclear umbrella' is a term used to describe security arrangements between nuclear States and non-nuclear States, whereby the non-nuclear State relies on 'extended nuclear deterrence arrangements with a nuclear-armed patron from whom they have received a nuclear security guarantee': Tytti Erästö, 'The Role of Umbrella States in the Global Nuclear Order' (*SIPRI Insights on Peace and Security*, No 2023/06, June 2023), 1, www.sipri.org/publications/2023/sipri-insights-peace-and-security/role-umbrella-states-global-nuclear-order. Non-nuclear States party to such arrangements are often called 'umbrella States'.

88 *NATO 2022 Strategic Concept*, adopted by heads of state and government at the NATO Summit in Madrid, 29 June 2022, www.nato.int/cps/en/natohq/topics_210907.htm.

89 *NATO 2022*, 1.

90 *NATO 2022*, 20.

91 *NATO 2022*, 20.

92 See, for example, the NC3 of Türkiye: Can Kasapoğlu, 'Turkey and Nuclear Command, Control and Communications' (*Tech4GS Special Reports*, 27 June 2019), https://securityandtechnology.org/wp-content/uploads/2024/10/kasapoglu_turkey_nc3_IST-1.pdf.

93 Peter Hayes, Binoy Kampmark, Philip Reiner, and Deborah Gordon, 'Synthesis Report, NC3 Systems and Strategic Stability: A Global Overview' (*Tech4GS Special Reports*, 6 May 2019), 25, https://securityandtechnology.org/wp-content/uploads/2024/10/nc3_synthesis_report_may_6_2019_IST.pdf.

94 Security Treaty between Australia, New Zealand, and the United States of America, 1 September 1951, entered into force 29 April 1952, 131 UNTS 84.

as such.[95] It should be noted that, notwithstanding the intent of ANZUS, the position regarding the alliance changed in the 1980s – at least in relation to the US–New Zealand relationship. Prior to 1987, Australia and New Zealand considered themselves under the US nuclear umbrella.[96] However, New Zealand passed domestic legislation in the 1980s[97] banning nuclear-powered ships from entering its territorial waters and prohibiting the acquisition, stationing, and testing of nuclear explosive devices in New Zealand's territory – a law that remains in place to this day.[98] In response, the United States suspended its obligations toward New Zealand under ANZUS,[99] though it maintains that the agreement has not been formally terminated as between the United States and New Zealand.[100]

- Bilateral and multilateral security agreements between nuclear States and Japan,[101] the Republic of Korea,[102] and Armenia, Belarus, Kazakhstan, Kyrgyzstan, Tajikistan, and Ukraine.[103]

2.3 Current Challenges for NC3 – Modernizing Legacy Systems and Threats Posed by Cyberattacks and AI

Finally, note should be made of two distinct though interrelated challenges that present themselves in the context of NC3: the modernization of existing legacy systems and the place of cyber and artificial intelligence (AI) in NC3 systems.

95 Australian Government Department of Defence, '2016 Defence White Paper' (2016), para 5.20, www.defence.gov.au/about/strategic-planning/defence-white-paper.

96 See Andrew Kelly, *ANZUS and the Early Cold War: Strategy and Diplomacy Between Australia, New Zealand and the United States, 1945–1956* (Open Book, 2018), 51–70; W David McIntyre, *Background to the ANZUS Pact: Policy-Making, Strategy and Diplomacy, 1945–55* (Palgrave Macmillan, 1995).

97 New Zealand Nuclear-Free Zone, Disarmament, and Arms Control Act 1987.

98 See New Zealand Foreign Affairs and Trade, 'The Nuclear Non-Proliferation Treaty (NPT)', www.mfat.govt.nz/en/peace-rights-and-security/disarmament/weapons-of-mass-destruction#bookmark0.

99 See Amy L Catalinac, 'Why New Zealand Took Itself Out of ANZUS: Observing "Opposition for Autonomy" in Asymmetric Alliances' (2010) 6 *Foreign Policy Analysis* 317, 318–319.

100 See US Department of State, Office of the Historian, 'The Australia, New Zealand and United States Security Treaty (ANZUS Treaty), 1951', https://history.state.gov/milestones/1945-1952/anzus.

101 Treaty of Mutual Cooperation and Security between the United States and Japan, 19 January 1960, entered into force 23 June 1960, 11 UST 1632.

102 Mutual Defense Treaty between the United States and the Republic of Korea, 1 October 1953, entered into force 17 November 1954, 238 UNTS 199.

103 Charter of the Collective Security Treaty Organization (7 October 2002), https://en.odkb-csto.org/documents/documents/ustav_organizatsii_dogovora_o_kollektivnoy_bezopasnosti_/#loaded.

2.3.1 Modernization and the Problems of Legacy NC3 Architecture

For most existing nuclear weapons States, NC3 systems are based on so-called legacy systems (i.e., old analog systems sit alongside digital systems) onto which nuclear States 'are superimposing and grafting on rapidly emerging technologies including drones, cyberwarfare, and highly automated data processing now moving into artificial intelligence and early applications of quantum computing and communications'.[104] The amalgamation of legacy and new systems creates fertile ground for systems errors and vulnerabilities that could lead to, for example, false positive launch warnings or inadvertent or unauthorized launches.[105]

However, even newer NC3 systems are not impervious to exploitable vulnerabilities – particularly the risks that NC3 integrity could be jeopardized by cyberattacks. Possible cyberattacks against NC3 could include spoofing[106] or jamming[107] early warning radars and satellites, either to deceptively convince a target that an attack is incoming, to block telemetry of an actual incoming attack so the target is caught unaware, or to misdirect attention from the attacking State such that the targeted State believes that the attack is coming from another source (that is, not the actual attacker). Other kinds of cyberattacks could result in unauthorized or accidental launches (or failed launches) of nuclear weapons following attacks on NC3 computer architecture. Finally, mistargeting or guidance failure of otherwise legitimate and lawful launches of nuclear weapons might result from cyberattacks against NC3 telemetry.[108]

104 Hayes, 'Nuclear Command, Control, and Communications (NC3) in Asia-Pacific'. See also Peter Hayes, 'Nuclear Command-and-Control in the Quantum Era' (*NAPSNet Blue Peter*, 29 March 2018), https://nautilus.org/napsnet/nuclear-command-and-control-in-the-quantum-era/.

105 For examples of system vulnerabilities and possible outcomes, see, for example, Harvey, 'U.S. Nuclear Command and Control for the 21st Century', 10.

106 Spoofing is when a hacker fakes the sending address of a transmission to gain illegal entry into a secure system or to otherwise deceptively convince the person or institution on the receiving end that the transmission is legitimate and to take action based on false assumptions or information. See further National Institute of Standards and Technology, 'spoofing', Computer Security and Resource Centre, https://csrc.nist.gov/glossary/term/spoofing.

107 Jamming is a 'deliberate communications disruption meant to degrade the operational performance of the [radio frequency] subsystem. Jamming is achieved by interjecting electromagnetic waves on the same frequency that the reader to tag uses for communication': National Institute of Standards and Technology, 'jamming', Computer Security and Resource Centre, https://csrc.nist.gov/glossary/term/jamming.

108 For a more detailed examination of the kinds of cyber vulnerabilities, see Jon Lindsay, 'Cyber Operations and Nuclear Weapons' (*Tech4GS Special Reports*, 20 June 2019); Page O Stoutland and Samantha Pitts-Kiefer, 'Nuclear Weapons in the New Cyber Age: Report of the Cyber-Nuclear Weapons Study Group' (*Nuclear Threat Initiative*, September 2018); Beyza Unal and Patricia Lewis, 'Cybersecurity of Nuclear Weapons Systems: Threats, Vulnerabilities, and Consequences' (*Chatham House*, January 2018).

2.3.2 Threats Posed by the Introduction of AI into NC3 Architecture

The rise of AI also presents unique threats with which any NC3 system must grapple.[109] AI offers appealing strategic benefits for armed forces relating to weaponry and targeting and has proven itself to be capable of the kinds of data retrieval and analysis that are beyond what humans can achieve on their own. It is able to 'source massive amounts of data across a complex network, process that data at machine speed, and then output a simple, understandable recommendation to human operators – or in some circumstances execute tasks without any human involvement'.[110] For armed forces preparing for and during armed conflict, the ability to acquire, process, analyze, and act on pertinent data at faster-than-human speed presents obvious strategic advantages – the ability to act at faster-than-human speeds during heightened security situations, where timely decision-making is critical (for instance, when a weapon is incoming), is clearly a strategic plus.

As noted by SIPRI, the employment of AI in such heightened security situations presents unique challenges, particularly in the nuclear realm.[111] An artificially intelligent and autonomous nuclear weapons system could fail catastrophically if it were operating in response to insufficient or corrupted data (example: if data was incomprehensible to the AI algorithm or if the AI [or those executing its decisions] were subject to biased decision-making processes.)[112] As noted by Hruby and Miller, these biases include

> human decision makers placing too little or too much trust in AI results, referred to as either a 'trust gap' or 'automation bias', respectively. The other type of bias is associated with inherent bias in data sets or rulemaking that is transferred from human behavior, likely unwittingly,[113]

such as gender or racial biases.[114] An example could be where the AI inaccurately identified a non-military vessel or vehicle as a threat (or failed to

109 See Jill Hruby and M Nina Miller, 'Assessing and Managing the Benefits and Risks of Artificial Intelligence in Nuclear-Weapon Systems' (*Nuclear Threat Initiative*, 2021).

110 Future of Life Institute, 'Risks of Artificial Intelligence in Nuclear Command, Control and Communications (NC3): Primer & Policy Options for Risk Mitigation' (July 2023), 2, https://futureoflife.org/fli_ai_nc3_policy_primer/.

111 See Vincent Boulanin, Lora Saalman, Petr Topychkanov, Fei Su, and Moa Peldán Carlsson, 'Artificial Intelligence, Strategic Stability and Nuclear Risk' (*SIPRI*, 2020), www.sipri.org/publications/2020/policy-reports/artificial-intelligence-strategic-stability-and-nuclear-risk.

112 Hruby and Miller, 'Assessing and Managing the Benefits and Risks of Artificial Intelligence in Nuclear-Weapon Systems', 7–8.

113 Hruby and Miller, 'Assessing and Managing the Benefits and Risks of Artificial Intelligence in Nuclear-Weapon Systems', 8.

114 Hruby and Miller, but see also Australian Human Rights Commission, 'Using Artificial Intelligence to Make Decisions: Addressing the Problem of Algorithmic Bias' (2020), https://humanrights.gov.au/our-work/technology-and-human-rights/publications/technical-paper-addressing-algorithmic-bias.

accurately identify a threat as a threat). As noted in recent research undertaken by SIPRI:

> Bias in military AI often manifests in more complex and subtle ways than portrayed in policy debates. Beyond gender and racial bias, military AI systems are likely to contain biases around, for example, disability status, age, socio-economic class, language, and culture. If these biases go unaddressed, they may undermine compliance with key IHL principles of *distinction*, *proportionality*, and, especially, *precautions in attack*.[115]

New technologies thus add an additional layer of complexity to the process of designing fit-for-purpose NC3 systems, which makes the need to seek clarity in NC3 systems all the more pressing. To that end, the next chapter will turn to look at the relevant international law that applies to nuclear operations, in order to understand the legal framework in which nuclear operations must be conducted.

115 Laura Bruun and Marta Bo, '"Constant Care" Must Be Taken to Address Bias in Military AI', *Humanitarian Law & Policy* (28 August 2025), https://blogs.icrc.org/law-and-policy/2025/08/28/constant-care-must-be-taken-to-address-bias-in-military-ai/.

3 Existing General International Laws and NC3

To properly understand NC3 systems and their operation, we also need to understand the background international legal framework. NC3 is the descriptor for the framework of the 'integrated system comprised of facilities, equipment, communications, procedures and personnel'[1] for a nuclear weapons (or nuclear weapons–sharing) State. Most simply, it is the complex multilayered system that governs the process that begins with the decision to launch a nuclear weapon (or weapons) to the final outcome of physically deploying the weapon.

NC3 in any State is governed by several levels of international and domestic law and policy, but in international law, there is no specific mention of NC3 *qua* NC3 in any extant treaty. The absence of explicit reference to NC3 does not, however, mean it is ungoverned by international law. Rather, several existing international law treaties, as well as a body of customary law, have direct relevance for any NC3 system. These treaties and customary law are examined in the next section of this chapter and relate to the general international law obligations that exist for the State (including, in particular, rights and obligations under principles of sovereignty, the rules of State responsibility, the law of neutrality, and the various nuclear weapons–specific treaties with regard to matters such as non-proliferation and test bans). That discussion will be followed in chapters 4, 5, and 6 on the law governing the use of force, the law of armed conflict including weapons law, and international criminal law, respectively.

3.1 Sovereignty and Jurisdiction

At the heart of any international law obligation – and thus any NC3 architecture – are several fundamental principles of international law. The first of these is that States enjoy sovereignty over their territory. Sovereignty over

1 US Air Force, *Air Force Nuclear Command, Control, and Communications (NC3)*, Air Force Instruction 13–550 (16 April 2019), 4.

DOI: 10.4324/9781003759294-3

territory imparts sovereign authority to govern activities that take place on that territory (by way of enacting and enforcing laws and regulations).[2] Therefore, with regard to nuclear weapons and NC3, States have sovereignty over any 'nuclear weapons and facilities that are located on their territory and over any activities that are connected with such weapons and facilities'.[3] States therefore have:

> [t]he sovereign right and, arguably, responsibility to enact legislation to prescribe which nuclear-weapons related activities are prohibited, to criminalise prohibited activities, to provide for the arrangements that are needed to secure nuclear weapons sites and equipment and the information related to nuclear weapons and to implement other necessary arrangements. In short, it will be pursuant to a nation's sovereign rights and responsibilities that NC3 procedures will be developed, applied and enforced.[4]

Sovereignty is not absolute: There are certain limits on State sovereignty that may restrict what a State can do – for example, with regard to persons and property entitled to State or diplomatic immunity, as well as limitations under the UN Convention on the Law of the Sea.[5]

A State may also, in accordance with international law, exercise jurisdiction over nuclear weapons and nuclear weapons operations on its territory – again, this is limited by other international law obligations (for example, pre-existing immunities, such as sovereign or diplomatic immunity). Exercising jurisdiction over nuclear weapons and nuclear weapons operations depends on being able to prove a jurisdictional link, either through the weapons or operations being located on a State's territory; by having a connection with the State due to 'the nationality of the person undertaking the [nuclear] operation', 'the nationality of the victim', or 'the threat that the operation creates to the national security of the State';[6] or because the activity triggers universal jurisdiction as it amounts to, for instance, an act of torture under the Torture Convention.[7] Jurisdiction is not limited to land territory; it may also

2 Samantha Besson, 'Sovereignty', *Max Planck Encyclopedia of Public International Law* (April 2011).

3 William H Boothby and Wolff Heintschel von Heinegg, *The Law on Nuclear Weapons: An International Commentary* (Edward Elgar, 2025), 52.

4 Boothby and Heintschel von Heinegg, *The Law on Nuclear Weapons*, 53.

5 For example, the right of innocent passage under the law of the sea: United Nations Convention on the Law of the Sea, opened for signature 10 December 1982, entered into force 16 November 1994, 1833 UNTS 3 (UNCLOS), arts 17–19, 37–38, 52–53.

6 William H Boothby and Wolff Heintschel von Heinegg, *Nuclear Weapons Law: Where Are We Now?* (Cambridge University Press, 2022), 18.

7 Convention against Torture and Other Cruel, Inhuman or Degrading Treatment or Punishment, opened for signature 10 December 1984, entered into force 26 June 1987, 1465 UNTS 85, arts 2, 4, 5.

encompass ships, aircraft, or other platforms, such as those located on the high seas, in which case, jurisdiction is connected to the flag State of the vessel or the State of registration.[8]

3.2 State Responsibility

Also central to the general international framework governing NC3 are the principles underpinning the rules on State responsibility. A State is responsible for any breaches of international law attributable to that State,[9] even if such acts are carried out contrary to instructions or in excess of authority.[10] It is therefore the responsibility of the State to ensure that any person acting on behalf of the State, under either the instructions or the direction or control of the State, is properly and appropriately supervised. Such supervision should extend to the provision of training and the implementation of proper disciplinary arrangements for members of the armed forces, as well as for any person serving in security or intelligence roles that may be connected to NC3 or nuclear weapons–related duties.

Finally, States must not allow their territory to be used for acts that adversely and unlawfully affect other States.[11] States are under an obligation to take suitable steps to protect the rights of other States, which can be considered as part of the general requirement of due diligence[12] – the requirement for States to take reasonable and appropriate steps 'to prevent or minimise'[13] harm to other States' interests. Due diligence is not so much a rigid standard – it differs in the various fields of international law (such as international investment law and international environmental law) – but, in the context of NC3, it would mean that States must take steps to minimize the risk of accidental or

8 Boothby and Heintschel von Heinegg, *The Law on Nuclear Weapons*, 58. See also UNCLOS, art 94.

9 Articles on the Responsibility of States for Internationally Wrongful Acts (ARSIWA), in International Law Commission, *Report of the International Law Commission on the Work of Its Fifty-third Session (23 April–1 June and 2 July–10 August 2001)*, UN Doc A/56/10 (2001), art 4: 'The conduct of any State organ shall be considered an act of that State under international law, whether the organ exercises legislative, executive, judicial or any other functions, whatever position it holds in the organization of the State, and whatever its character as an organ of the central Government or of a territorial unit of the State'; art 8: 'The conduct of a person or group of persons shall be considered an act of a State under international law if the person or group of persons is in fact acting on the instructions of, or under the direction or control of, that State in carrying out the conduct'.

10 ARSIWA, art 7.

11 *Corfu Channel (United Kingdom v Albania)*, Judgment, 1949 ICJ Rep 4 (9 April), 22.

12 *United States Diplomatic and Consular Staff in Tehran (United States of America v Iran)*, Judgment, 1980 ICJ Rep 3 (24 May), paras 67–68 (though, in this case, it is discussed in terms of due diligence obligations arising under treaty law).

13 Anne Peters, Heike Krieger, and Leonhard Kreuzer, 'Due Diligence in International Law: Dissecting the Leitmotif of Current Accountability Debates', in Heike Krieger, Anne Peters, and Leonhard Kreuzer (eds), *Due Diligence in the International Legal Order* (Oxford University Press, 2020), 5.

negligent access to, or launching of, nuclear weapons. It might also form the basis of an obligation to warn States of an inadvertent incoming strike.

3.3 The Law of Neutrality

Neutrality law is codified in the 1907 Hague Conventions V[14] and XIII,[15] which remain the most relevant treaties on the subject. The law of neutrality provides that, upon commencement of an armed conflict, all States not party to the conflict must choose whether to remain separate from or join in the hostilities with specific rights and obligations that follow consequent to such a choice. States that choose to abstain from hostilities must have that neutrality respected, most obviously by their territory remaining inviolable. Neutral States may not be attacked[16] and belligerent parties must respect the neutrality of such nations. However, to enjoy that neutrality, a neutral State must:

- abstain from participating in the conflict by not engaging in acts of hostility against parties to the conflict and not allow its territory to be used in any way by parties to the conflict;
- remain impartial and not show any preference to any belligerent State, though pre-existing commercial and treaty arrangements may continue undisturbed; and
- defend its neutrality by defending itself against violations of that neutrality, even by force if necessary.

In the context of nuclear warfare and nuclear weapons, it is generally accepted[17] that parties to an armed conflict must take all feasible measures to ensure that no harmful effects have an impact on neutral territory. However, this rule is not found in the Hague Conventions – rather, it is derived from the general international law obligation on States to refrain from acts that violate the rights of other States. Therefore, a nuclear-launching State would have to be aware of the degree to which, for instance, the release of radiation following a nuclear attack would impact neutral States.

3.4 Nuclear Weapons–Specific Treaties

This study now turns to look at the international and regional treaties that deal specifically with the threat and/or use of nuclear weapons and would

14 Convention (V) Respecting the Rights and Duties of Neutral Powers and Persons in Case of War on Land, 18 October 1907, 36 Stat 2310 (Hague Convention V).

15 Convention (XIII) Concerning the Rights and Duties of Neutral Powers in Naval War, 18 October 1907, 36 Stat 2415.

16 Hague Convention V, art 1.

17 Boothby and Heintschel von Heinegg, *The Law on Nuclear Weapons*, 231.

need to be considered in the framework of any NC3 infrastructure. These are, primarily, the Treaty on the Prohibition of Nuclear Weapons (TPNW)[18] and the Treaty on the Non-Proliferation of Nuclear Weapons (NPT),[19] which are joined by multilateral treaties that prohibit, inter alia, nuclear weapons tests in specific circumstances or designated geographical areas.[20] These treaties are joined by bilateral nuclear weapons limitation treaties adopted between the United States and Russia,[21] as well as regional treaties on nuclear weapon–free zones. As with all treaties at international law, States are only bound under treaties they have ratified.

3.4.1 Treaty on the Prohibition of Nuclear Weapons

The TPNW, in Article 1, provides:

1. Each State Party undertakes never under any circumstances to:

   (a) Develop, test, produce, manufacture, otherwise acquire, possess or stockpile nuclear weapons or other nuclear explosive devices;
   (b) Transfer to any recipient whatsoever nuclear weapons or other nuclear explosive devices or control over such weapons or explosive devices directly or indirectly;
   (c) Receive the transfer of or control over nuclear weapons or other nuclear explosive devices directly or indirectly;
   (d) Use or threaten to use nuclear weapons or other nuclear explosive devices;
   (e) Assist, encourage or induce, in any way, anyone to engage in any activity prohibited to a State Party under this Treaty;

18 Treaty on the Prohibition of Nuclear Weapons, 20 September 2017, entered into force 22 January 2021, 3379 UNTS 1 (TPNW).

19 Treaty on the Non-Proliferation of Nuclear Weapons, 1 July 1968, entered into force 5 March 1970, 729 UNTS 161 (NPT).

20 See, for example, Treaty Banning Nuclear Weapon Tests in the Atmosphere, in Outer Space and Under Water, opened for signature 8 August 1963, entered into force 10 October 1963, 480 UNTS 43; Treaty on the Prohibition of the Emplacement of Nuclear Weapons and Other Weapons of Mass Destruction on the Sea-Bed and the Ocean Floor and in the Subsoil Thereof, opened for signature 11 February 1971, entered into force 18 May 1972, 955 UNTS 115.

21 Including the Treaty between the United States of America and the Russian Federation on Measures for the Further Reduction and Limitation of Strategic Offensive Arms, Prague, 8 April 2010 (New START). The duration of New START was limited until 5 February 2021. In January 2021, the parties agreed on an extension for a further five years. Defunct treaties between the two States include the Treaty between the United States of America and the Union of Soviet Socialist Republics on the Elimination of Their Intermediate-Range and Shorter-Range Missiles, Washington, 8 December 1987, (INF Treaty) and the Treaty on the Limitation of Anti-Ballistic Missile Systems, Moscow, 26 May 1972 (ABM Treaty). Because of the withdrawal of the United States, the INF Treaty expired on 2 August 2019. The United States also withdrew from the ABM Treaty, thus terminating the Treaty as of June 2002.

(f) Seek or receive any assistance, in any way, from anyone to engage in any activity prohibited to a State Party under this Treaty;
(g) Allow any stationing, installation or deployment of any nuclear weapons or other nuclear explosive devices in its territory or at any place under its jurisdiction or control.

Only one State that is, in theory, under the nuclear umbrella of other States has signed the TPNW: Kazakhstan. (New Zealand is also party to the TPNW, but, as noted previously, it is not under the US nuclear umbrella.)[22] Australia has recently indicated that it is exploring whether it can sign the TPNW and remain under the US nuclear umbrella as part of ANZUS.[23]

3.4.2 Treaty on the Non-Proliferation of Nuclear Weapons

Under Article 1 of the NPT, obligations for the nuclear weapons States include the following:

> Each nuclear-weapon State Party to the Treaty undertakes not to transfer to any recipient whatsoever nuclear weapons or other nuclear explosive devices or control over such weapons or explosive devices directly, or indirectly; and not in any way to assist, encourage, or induce any non-nuclear-weapon State to manufacture or otherwise acquire nuclear weapons or other nuclear explosive devices, or control over such weapons or explosive devices.

This injunction is joined by Article III(2), which provides:

> Each State Party to the Treaty undertakes not to provide: (a) source or special fissionable material, or (b) equipment or material especially designed or prepared for the processing, use or production of special fissionable material, to any non-nuclear-weapon State for peaceful purposes, unless the source or special fissionable material shall be subject to the safeguards required by this Article.

All nuclear States and nuclear umbrella States, with the exception of India, Israel, and Pakistan, are party to the NPT.

There is notable controversy regarding the participation of nuclear umbrella States in the NPT – specifically, that it is antithetical for States

22 Note that Article 18 provides that the TPNW does not prejudice the application of other pre-existing international law agreements, so long as those obligations are consistent with the Treaty – this would presumably include pre-existing obligations under security arrangement treaties.
23 See further ICAN, 'Australia's Reassessment of the Treaty on the Prohibition of Nuclear Weapons' (15 November 2022), www.icanw.org/australia_tpnw.

to denounce proliferation as provided under the NPT while simultaneously benefitting from an alliance or other binding assurance that nuclear weapons could be used in their defence. Additionally, the doctrine of nuclear deterrence – the idea that only by possessing nuclear weapons can their non-use be ensured – is:

> the source of constant tension among NPT states parties. The need to deter conflict as much as possible is not contentious. What is at issue, in the view of many non-nuclear weapon states, is the threat of use of nuclear weapons to deter aggression. Deployment of such destructive and inherently indiscriminate armaments is regarded by those states as incompatible with international humanitarian law. Failure of the doctrine of nuclear deterrence, as already noted, could entail a humanitarian tragedy of regional, if not, global consequence, with disproportionate civilian casualties.[24]

The position on the compatibility between extended deterrence and NPT obligations thus remains a live issue.

3.4.3 Comprehensive Test Ban Treaty

Under the Comprehensive Test Ban Treaty:

> 1. Each State Party undertakes not to carry out any nuclear weapon test explosion or any other nuclear explosion, and to prohibit and prevent any such nuclear explosion at any place under its jurisdiction or control.
> 2. Each State Party undertakes, furthermore, to refrain from causing, encouraging, or in any way participating in the carrying out of any nuclear weapon test explosion or any other nuclear explosion.[25]

However, the Comprehensive Test Ban Treaty has not yet entered into force. While a number of the nuclear weapons States have signed the instrument, only France and the United Kingdom have ratified it.[26] The Treaty will only enter into force once all States listed in Annex II have done so – those States include Algeria, Argentina, Australia, Austria, Bangladesh, Belgium, Brazil,

24 Yasmin Afina and Tim Caughley, 'NATO and the Frameworks of Nuclear Non-proliferation and Disarmament: Challenges for the 10th NPT Review Conference' (*Research Paper, Chatham House*, 29 May 2020), www.chathamhouse.org/2020/05/nato-and-frameworks-nuclear-non-proliferation-and-disarmament/1-introduction.

25 UN General Assembly, *Resolution 50/245: Comprehensive Nuclear-Test-Ban Treaty*, UN Doc A/RES/50/245 (17 September 1996), which adopted *Letter Dated 22 August 1996 from the Permanent Representative of Australia to the United Nations Addressed to the Secretary-General*, UN Doc A/50/1027 (26 August 1996), annex (Draft Comprehensive Nuclear-Test-Ban Treaty), art I.

26 See further UN Treaty Collection, 'Comprehensive Nuclear-Test-Ban Treaty', https://treaties.un.org/pages/ViewDetails.aspx?src=TREATY&mtdsg_no=XXVI-4&chapter=26.

Bulgaria, Canada, Chile, China, Colombia, the Democratic People's Republic of the Congo, the DPRK, Egypt, Finland, France, Germany, Hungary, India, Indonesia, the Islamic Republic of Iran, Israel, Italy, Japan, Mexico, the Netherlands, Norway, Pakistan, Peru, Poland, Romania, the Republic of Korea, the Russian Federation, Slovakia, South Africa, Spain, Sweden, Switzerland, Türkiye, Ukraine, the United Kingdom, the United States, and Vietnam. The necessity of ratification from the DPRK, India, Israel, and Pakistan seems to guarantee that the Treaty will not come into force as it currently stands.

3.4.4 Regional Nuclear Weapon–Free Zone Treaties

Joining these nuclear weapons–specific treaties are several regional treaties that establish nuclear weapon–free zones: the Treaty of Tlatelolco,[27] which creates a nuclear-weapon–free zone in Latin America and the Caribbean; the Treaty of Rarotonga,[28] which sets up a nuclear weapon–free zone in the South Pacific; the Treaty of Bangkok,[29] which covers Southeast Asia; the Treaty of Pelindaba,[30] which establishes a nuclear weapon–free zone in Africa; and the Treaty on a Nuclear Weapon–Free Zone in Central Asia.[31] Mongolia has also declared itself a nuclear weapon–free State.[32]

These treaties, as a general principle, prohibit parties from possessing, producing, or acquiring nuclear weapons.[33] Notably, the treaties also come with protocols, which provide that protocol parties agree not to use or threaten the use of a nuclear explosive device against any party to the treaty or any territory in the nuclear weapon–free zone.[34] Several nuclear weapons States are party to such protocols, which would mean that the NC3 of any specific

27 Treaty for the Prohibition of Nuclear Weapons in Latin America and the Caribbean, opened for signature 14 February 1967, entered into force 22 April 1968, 634 UNTS 281 (Treaty of Tlatelolco).

28 South Pacific Nuclear Free Zone Treaty, opened for signature 6 August 1985, entered into force 11 December 1986, 1445 UNTS 177.

29 Treaty on the Southeast Asia Nuclear Weapon-Free Zone, opened for signature 15 December 1995, entered into force 27 March 1997, 1981 UNTS 129.

30 African Nuclear Weapon–Free Zone Treaty, opened for signature 12 April 1996, entered into force 15 July 2009, 35 ILM 698 (Treaty of Pelindaba).

31 Treaty on a Nuclear Weapon–Free Zone Treaty in Central Asia, opened for signature 8 September 2006, entered into force 21 March 2009, 2970 UNTS 91.

32 See further United Nations, 'Mongolia's Nuclear-Weapon-Free Status', www.un.org/nwfz/content/mongolias-nuclear-weapon-free-status.

33 This fact is acknowledged in the preamble to the Treaty on a Nuclear Weapon–Free Zone Treaty in Central Asia: *Recognizing* that a number of regions, including Latin America and the Caribbean, the South Pacific, South-East Asia and Africa, have created nuclear-weapon-free zones, in which the possession of nuclear weapons, their development, production, introduction and deployment as well as use or threat of use, are prohibited'.

34 See, for example, Protocol I to the Treaty of Pelindaba, art 1: 'Each Protocol Party undertakes not to use or threaten to use a nuclear explosive device against: (a) Any Party to the Treaty; or

nuclear weapons State would need to take into account any such obligations contained in those protocols – for example, Protocol I of the Treaty of the Tlatelolco obliges States outside the Treaty zone to 'apply the denuclearization provisions of the Treaty to the territories in the zone "for which de jure or de facto they are internationally responsible"'.[35] France, the Netherlands, the United Kingdom, and the United States accepted the obligation in relation to their own territories, which, for the United States, include Puerto Rico, the US Virgin Islands, and the naval base at Guantanamo Bay.

3.4.5 Nuclear Weapons–Specific Provisions in International Law Treaties

Finally, there are two other key international treaties that contain provisions relating to nuclear weapons and impose limitations on the use and placement of such weapons. The Outer Space Treaty,[36] in Article IV, provides:

> States Parties to the Treaty undertake not to place in orbit around the earth any objects carrying nuclear weapons or any other kinds of weapons of mass destruction, install such weapons on celestial bodies, or station such weapons in outer space in any other manner.
>
> The moon and other celestial bodies shall be used by all States Parties to the Treaty exclusively for peaceful purposes. The establishment of military bases, installations and fortifications, the testing of any type of weapons and the conduct of military manoeuvres on celestial bodies shall be forbidden. The use of military personnel for scientific research or for any other peaceful purposes shall not be prohibited. The use of any equipment or facility necessary for peaceful exploration of the moon and other celestial bodies shall also not be prohibited.

Many of the nuclear weapons and nuclear umbrella States are party to the Outer Space Treaty, including China, France, India, Israel, Pakistan, Russia, the United Kingdom, and the United States.

Similarly, the Antarctic Treaty[37] provides in Article I that 'Antarctica shall be used for peaceful purposes only. There shall be prohibited, *inter alia*, any

---

(b) Any territory within the African nuclear-weapon-free zone for which a State that has become a Party to Protocol III is internationally responsible as defined in Annex I'.

35 US Department of State, 'Treaty for the Prohibition of Nuclear Weapons in Latin America and the Caribbean (Treaty of Tlatelolco)', https://2009-2017.state.gov/t/isn/4796.htm.

36 Treaty on Principles Governing the Activities of States in the Exploration and Use of Outer Space, including the Moon and Other Celestial Bodies, opened for signature 27 January 1967, entered into force 10 October 1967, 610 UNTS 205 (Outer Space Treaty).

37 Antarctic Treaty, opened for signature 1 December 1959, entered into force 23 June 1961, 402 UNTS 71.

measures of a military nature, such as the establishment of military bases and fortifications, the carrying out of military maneuvers, as well as the testing of any type of weapons' and in Article V that '[a]ny nuclear explosions in Antarctica and the disposal there of radioactive waste material shall be prohibited'. Nuclear weapons States party to the Antarctic Treaty include France, Russia, the United Kingdom, and the United States.

Given that these regional and subject-specific treaties include prohibitions on the use and/or stationing of nuclear weapons, it follows that any NC3 system would have to consider the relevant operative provisions if the NC3 State in question is party to those treaties.

4 The Law on the Use of Force

To determine whether the use of nuclear weapons might ever be considered legal, we must examine established international law on the use of force (codified in the 1945 Charter of the United Nations[1] but also exists as a distinct body of customary international law).[2] The UN Charter was adopted near the end of the Second World War, enshrining into international law a prohibition on the use or threat of force by one State against another.

4.1 The General Prohibition on the Use of Force in International Law

Article 2(4) of the UN Charter provides:

> All Members shall refrain in their international relations from the threat or use of force against the territorial integrity or political independence of any state, or in any other manner inconsistent with the Purposes of the United Nations.

Article 2(4) is not an absolute prohibition – States are permitted to use force (a) in self-defence[3] or (b) pursuant to action authorized by the Security Council.[4]

1 Opened for signature 26 June 1945, entered into force 24 October 1945, XV UNCIO 355 (UN Charter).

2 *Military and Paramilitary Activities in and against Nicaragua (Nicaragua v United States of America)*, Jurisdiction and Admissibility, 1984 ICJ Rep 392 (26 November), para 73; *Military and Paramilitary Activities in and against Nicaragua, (Nicaragua v United States of America)*, Merits, Judgment, 1986 ICJ Rep 14 (27 June) (*Nicaragua Merits*), paras 187–190; *Legal Consequences of the Construction of a Wall in the Occupied Palestinian Territory*, Advisory Opinion, 2004 ICJ Rep 136 (9 July) (*Israeli Wall*), para 87.

3 UN Charter, art 51.

4 Pursuant to UN Charter, arts 39, 42.

DOI: 10.4324/9781003759294-4

The UN Charter binds all States party to the Charter, which, as of this writing, includes all States in the world.[5] The provisions of the Charter bind all parties, and, in the event of conflict between obligations under the Charter and any obligations that might exist under any other international agreement, Article 103 provides that Charter obligations prevail. Moreover, the prohibition on the use of force is also considered to be *jus cogens*, a peremptory norm, binding on all States and permitting no derogation.[6]

In addition to the Charter obligations regarding the use of force, States are also bound to the customary international law regarding force, which, as noted by the International Court of Justice (ICJ) in *Nicaragua v United States of America*, 'continues to exist alongside treaty law. The areas governed by the two sources of law . . . do not overlap exactly, and the rules do not have the same content'.[7] However, most of the literature notes that the obligations under the Charter regarding the use of force are, for the most part (though not absolutely), coextensive with those in custom.[8]

Turning now to the substance of Article 2(4), several aspects of the prohibition contained in that article should be noted. The prohibition on the threat or use of force exists only between States in 'their international relations' – Article 2(4) does not exist to prohibit the use or threat of force by a State in the context of domestic unrest or intra-State conflict.[9] Additionally, the prohibition of the threat or use exists against 'any State' – for example, there is no right to threaten or use force against any State, regardless of whether it is a member of the United Nations.[10]

Article 2(4) prohibits both threats of force and uses of force directed against the 'territorial integrity' or 'political independence' of another State. While the UN Charter does not define either term, State practice and the writings of scholars and practitioners have determined that, broadly speaking, territorial integrity relates to 'the territorial "oneness" or "wholeness" of the State' while political independence refers to the 'autonomy in the affairs of the State with respect to its institutions, freedom of political decisions,

5 See United Nations, 'Member States', www.un.org/en/about-us/member-states. Only the Holy See and Palestine are non-member States: see www.un.org/en/about-us/non-member-states.

6 International Law Commission, *Report of the International Law Commission on the Work of Its Seventy-first Session (29 April–7 June and 8 July–9 August 2019)*, UN Doc A/74/10 (2019), 141–208.

7 *Nicaragua Merits*, para 176.

8 See Russell Buchan and Nicholas Tsagourias, *Regulating the Use of Force in International Law: Stability and Change* (Edward Elgar, 2021), ch 2; Christine Gray, *International Law and the Use of Force* (4th ed, Oxford University Press, 2018), ch 1; Lindsay Moir, *Reappraising the Resort to Force: International Law, Jus ad Bellum and the War on Terror* (Hart, 2010), ch 1. For the purposes of this book, the focus will be on the law on the use of force as enshrined in the UN Charter.

9 There is contentious debate regarding whether there is a right to use force in self-defence against non-State actors. This is discussed further later in this chapter.

10 Though, as noted earlier, this is less of an issue as nearly all States in the world are UN members.

policy making, and in matters pertaining to its domestic and foreign affairs'.[11] Therefore, States must not threaten or use force to violate existing State boundaries or to annex territory and must not threaten or use force to intervene in the domestic affairs of another State to, for instance, politically influence or even overthrow an existing government.[12] Article 2(7) of the UN Charter reaffirms:

> Nothing contained in the present Charter shall authorize the United Nations to intervene in matters which are essentially within the domestic jurisdiction of any state or shall require the Members to submit such matters to settlement under the present Charter; but this principle shall not prejudice the application of enforcement measures under Chapter VII.

As international law prohibits the threat and/or use of force, it is necessary to define what is a threat of force and what is a use of force. Neither threat of force nor use of force is defined in the UN Charter, but through application of the rules of treaty interpretation and from examination of State practice, it is evident that 'force' in this context is intended to mean 'armed force'. The UN Charter makes clear that among its objectives is the aim 'to ensure . . . that armed force shall not be used, save in the common interest'.[13] That 'force' in the Charter must be taken to mean armed or military force is affirmed by recourse to the *travaux préparatoires*, where a proposal that the Article 2(4) prohibition include economic coercion was rejected.[14] This interpretation has been supported in State practice since 1945, when landmark instruments reaffirming the prohibition contained in Article 2(4) – such as the Friendly

11 Samuel KN Blay, 'Territorial Integrity and Political Independence', *Max Planck Encyclopedia of Public International Law* (March 2010), https://opil.ouplaw.com/display/10.1093/law:epil/9780199231690/law-9780199231690-e1116. See also UN General Assembly, *Resolution 1514 (XV): Declaration on the Granting of Independence to Colonial Countries and Peoples*, UN Doc A/RES/1514(XV) (14 December 1960); UN General Assembly, *Resolution 2625 (XXV): Declaration on Principles of International Law Concerning Friendly Relations and Co-operation Among States in Accordance with the Charter of the United Nations*, UN Doc 2625 (XXV) (24 October 1970) (UNGA Res 2625 (XXV)).

12 See, for example, UN General Assembly, *Resolution 2131 (XX): Declaration on the Inadmissibility of Intervention in the Domestic Affairs of States and the Protection of Their Independence and Sovereignty*, UN Doc A/RES/2131(XX) (21 December 1965); UN General Assembly, *Resolution 3314 (XXIX): Definition of Aggression*, UN Doc A/RES/3314(XXIX) (14 December 1974) (UNGA Res 3314 (XXIX)).

13 Preamble to the UN Charter, para 7.

14 For examples of State delegates discussing 'force' as meaning 'armed force', see United Nations, *Documents of the United Nations Conference on International Organization, San Francisco, 1945: Volume III* (United Nations Information Organizations, 1945), 70, 304, 334–335, 342–346, 356, 368, 400, 459. See also Bruno Simma, Daniel-Erasmus Khan, Georg Nolte, Andreas Paulus, and Nikolai Wessendorf (eds), *The Charter of the United Nations: A Commentary, Volume I* (3rd ed, Oxford University Press, 2012), 18.

Relations Declaration (1970)[15] – also adopt this definition of force as equating to armed force. Additionally, case law since 1970 has further enshrined the definition, where, for instance, the supply of funds to an insurgent group[16] and law enforcement actions against another State (for example, the boarding and inspection of a fishing vessel)[17] were not deemed to be use of force.

A State will violate the prohibition on the use of force if it uses direct force (that is, through its own military), but it will also breach the prohibition if it uses 'indirect force'. Indirect force is where a State uses a non-State group to carry out a use of force. As noted in the Friendly Relations Declaration, indirect uses of force include:

> organizing or encouraging the organization of irregular forces or armed bands, including mercenaries, for incursion into the territory of another State. . . . organizing, instigating, assisting or participating in acts of civil strife or terrorist acts in another State or acquiescing in organized activities within its territory directed towards the commission of such acts, when the acts referred to in the present paragraph involve a threat or use of force.[18]

A threat to use force is equally prohibited under international law.[19] Therefore, if a threat, if carried out, could be classified as a use of force, then the threat itself would be illegal.[20] However, to be unlawful, a threat must be specific – the mere acquisition or retention of weapons in itself would not be considered a threat.[21] As noted by the ICJ in the *Nuclear Weapons Advisory Opinion*, there must be 'a signalled intention to use force if certain events occur' or 'the declared readiness of a State to use force'.[22]

4.2 Permissible Exceptions to the Prohibition on the Use of Force

There are limited exceptions to the prohibition on the use of force – situations in which a use of force by one State against another will not be a breach of

15 UNGA Res 2625 (XXV).

16 *Nicaragua Merits*, para 228.

17 *Fisheries Jurisdiction (Spain v Canada)*, Jurisdiction, Judgment, 1998 ICJ Rep 432 (4 December), para 84.

18 UNGA Res 2625 (XXV).

19 *Legality of the Threat or Use of Nuclear Weapons*, Advisory Opinion, 1996 ICJ Rep 226 (8 July)), para 47.

20 Buchan and Tsagourias, *Regulating the Use of Force in International Law*, 33–35.

21 Buchan and Tsagourias, *Regulating the Use of Force in International Law*, 34.

22 *Nuclear Weapons Advisory Opinion*, para 47. See also *Guyana v Suriname*, Award, ICGJ 370 (PCA 2007), 17 September 2007, paras 432, 445, where the arbitral tribunal found that, in a situation where Surinamese Navy gunboats demanded that a Guyanese-licensed oil rig leave disputed waters, the statement that the oil rig 'leave the area in 12 hours [or] the consequences will be yours' was a threat of force.

international law. The first of these exceptions is found in the law of State responsibility: A State that has consent under international law to use force on the territory of another State has not breached the prohibition in Article 2(4) of the UN Charter. As outlined in Article 20 of the Articles on the Responsibility of States for Internationally Wrongful Acts,[23] '[v]alid consent by a State to the commission of a given act by another State precludes the wrongfulness of that act in relation to the former State to the extent that the act remains within the limits of that consent'.[24] Consent precludes the wrongfulness of an act that would otherwise be contrary to international law.[25] For example, when Russian military forces transited Belarusian territory in order to invade Ukraine in February 2022, the transit was, prima facie, a use of force by Russia against Belarus. However, Belarusian authorities had granted Russia permission to transit their territory, thus precluding the characterization of Russian acts as a use of force against Belarus.

However, the larger body of law regarding exceptions to the use of force relates to the law on self-defence. Article 51 of the UN Charter provides:

> Nothing in the present Charter shall impair the inherent right of individual or collective self-defence if an armed attack occurs against a Member of the United Nations, until the Security Council has taken measures necessary to maintain international peace and security. Measures taken by Members in the exercise of this right of self-defence shall be immediately reported to the Security Council and shall not in any way affect the authority and responsibility of the Security Council under the present Charter to take at any time such action as it deems necessary in order to maintain or restore international peace and security.

As with Article 2(4), Article 51 is considered customary law; the use of the term 'inherent right' has been affirmed by the ICJ as meaning that Article 51 preserved but did not displace a customary right of self-defence.[26]

A lawful use of force in self-defence requires observing certain rules. These include that the act in self-defence is carried out in response to an armed attack, that the response is necessary to repel the attack, and that the

23 Articles on the Responsibility of States for Internationally Wrongful Acts (ARSIWA), in International Law Commission, *Report of the International Law Commission on the Work of Its Fifty-third Session (23 April–1 June and 2 July–10 August 2001)*, UN Doc A/56/10 (2001).

24 See also James Crawford, *State Responsibility: The General Part* (Cambridge University Press, 2013), 283–289.

25 See *Armed Activities on the Territory of the Congo (Democratic Republic of the Congo v Uganda)*, Judgment, 2005 ICJ Rep 168 (19 December), para 52 (*Armed Activities*); Crawford, *State Responsibility*, 287; ARSIWA Commentary, in *Report of the International Law Commission on the Work of Its Fifty-third Session (23 April–1 June and 2 July–10 August 2001)*, UN Doc A/56/10 (2001), 73–74 (art 20), para 9.

26 *Nicaragua Merits*, para 176.

use of force is proportionate to repel the attack.[27] Under Article 51, an act of self-defence is required to be reported to the Security Council. Finally, if acting in collective self-defence (that is, the defence of another State), there must have been a declaration by the victim State that it has been the victim of an armed attack and was requesting assistance.[28]

As with the term 'use of force', there is no definition in the UN Charter for 'armed attack', and guidance must be sought from State practice and the practice of the ICJ. In the *Nicaragua* case, the ICJ held that an armed attack is an operation which, because of its 'scale and effects', is the 'most grave' form of the use of force – in contrast to, for example, a 'mere frontier incident'.[29] Therefore, all armed attacks are uses of force allowing for a use of force in response, but not all uses of force are armed attacks. Examples of armed attacks were enumerated in the UN General Assembly's definition of aggression, including an invasion, a bombardment, a blockade, and

> [t]he sending by or on behalf of a State of armed bands, groups, irregulars or mercenaries, which carry out acts of armed force against another State of such gravity as to amount to the acts listed above, or its substantial involvement therein.[30]

Article 51 frames the right of self-defence as arising 'if an armed attack occurs'. This phrasing has led to some debate regarding whether an armed attack must have already happened or be in progress before a lawful response can be implemented. Put another way, can a State lawfully respond to an imminent attack, or even an anticipated or predicted attack, or must the attack already have taken place? It seems generally accepted in practice that a use of force in response to a prior armed attack is considered retaliatory[31] and, therefore, outside the bounds of a defensive action. However, practice suggests that an *imminent* attack would allow for a lawful use of force in response, with

27 See Dapo Akande and Thomas Liefländer, 'Clarifying Necessity, Imminence, and Proportionality in the Law of Self-Defense' (2013) 107 *American Journal of International Law* 563; Chris O'Meara, *Necessity and Proportionality and the Right of Self-Defence in International Law* (Oxford University Press, 2021); Adil Ahmad Haque, 'Necessity and Proportionality in International Law', in Larry May (ed), *The Cambridge Handbook of the Just War* (Cambridge University Press, 2018).

28 See Article 21 of ARSIWA: 'The wrongfulness of an act of a State is precluded if the act constitutes a lawful measure of self-defence taken in conformity with the Charter of the United Nations'. 'Lawful' in this context refers to the law on self-defence as outlined in Article 51 of the UN Charter and customary rules on self-defence, such as requirements of necessity and proportionality. See further *Oil Platforms (Islamic Republic of Iran v United States of America)*, Judgment, 2003 ICJ Rep 161 (6 November) (*Oil Platforms*).

29 *Nicaragua Merits*, paras 191, 195,230. The provision of arms to the opposition in another State is also not an armed attack. See also *Oil Platforms*, para 51.

30 UNGA Res 3314 (XXIX), art 3.

31 See UNGA Res 2625 (XXV), Principle 1.

support being found in UN reports,[32] in State practice,[33] and in selected commentary from practitioners.[34]

Less accepted in practice is whether a lawful use of force is permissible in situations of predicted or inchoate armed attacks – that is, when a State perceives that it *might* be subject to an armed attack due to, for example, historical tensions with other States (for example, as between India and Pakistan)[35] and in the absence of intelligence to suggest that an attack is imminent. Examples of States claiming a right of pre-emptive self-defence against perceived threats are limited, with notable examples being Israel[36] and the United States.[37] Most States have rejected such a broad view of the right of self-defence.[38]

Two final points regarding the use of force and permissible exceptions should be noted. The first of these relates to the use of force against non-State actors. The UN Charter provides that the right to use force against non-State actors in self-defence arises when a State has been the victim of an armed attack. Traditionally, it was accepted that an armed attack could only come from another State.[39] The acts of a non-State group operating within that State could only trigger a right to respond in self-defence where the 'host' can be considered responsible for the attack, either because the attack is attributable

32 United Nations, *A More Secure World: Our Shared Responsibility, Report of the High-Level Panel on Threats, Challenges and Change* (United Nations, 2004), para 188; UN Secretary-General, *In Larger Freedom: Towards Development, Security and Human Rights for All*, UN Doc A/59/2005 (21 March 2005), para 124.

33 See the speech by the Australian attorney general, reprinted in George Brandis, 'The Right of Self-Defence Against Imminent Armed Attack in International Law' (2018) 35 *Australian Year Book of International Law* 55.

34 See Elizabeth Wilmshurst, 'Principles of International Law on the Use of Force by States in Self-Defence' (*Chatham House*, ILP WP 05/01, Royal Institute of International Affairs, 2005); Daniel Bethlehem, 'Principles Relevant to the Scope of a State's Right of Self-Defense Against an Imminent or Actual Armed Attack by Nonstate Actors' (2012) 106 *American Journal of International Law* 769.

35 See Varun Vaish, 'Negotiating the India-Pakistan Conflict in Relation to Kashmir' (2011) 28 *International Journal on World Peace* 53; Rathnam Indurthy, *India–Pakistan Wars and the Kashmir Crisis* (Routledge, 2019).

36 Such as Israeli attacks against chemical facilities in Syria in the years since 2011: see, for example, TOI Staff, 'Israeli Jets Said to Strike Iranian-Run Missile Production Facility in Syria', *Times of Israel* (22 July 2018), www.timesofisrael.com/israel-jets-said-to-strike-chemical-weapons-site-in-syria/.

37 United States, *National Security Strategy of the United States* (The White House, December 2017), 11.

38 The Non-Aligned Movement, for example, maintains its opposition. '[Members] *Oppose* and *condemn* . . . the adoption of the doctrine of pre-emptive attack, . . . which is inconsistent with international law': Non-Aligned Movement, *Ministerial Meeting of the Coordinating Bureau of the Non-Aligned Movement (CoB-NAM): Final Document*, NAM 2019/CoB/Doc.1 (2019), para 38.6.

39 *Israeli Wall*, para 139. See also *Armed Activities*, Separate Opinion of Judge Simma, paras 12–15; Separate Opinion of Judge Kooijmans, paras 25–29.

to the host State under the rules of State responsibility or because the State has 'sent' the armed group to attack the other State (within the meaning of Article 3(g) of the Definition of Aggression).[40] In the absence of a link between the armed group and the State, the victim State would, under the traditional view of the law on the use of force, be unable to lawfully respond.

However, since the 9/11 attacks against the United States in 2001, there has been emergent but increasing support for the notion that a victim State may have a right to respond with force on the territory of a State where a non-State group is operating, even absent a link with the territorial State. Article 51 does not expressly require the attack to be by a State – only that it is an armed attack. Furthermore, Security Council Resolutions 1368[41] and 1373,[42] concerning the 9/11 attacks, both referred in their preambles to 'the inherent right of individual or collective self-defence', without making reference to a requirement that a State be the victim of an attack by another State. Drawing on reasoning forwarded by Judges Kooijmans and Simma in *Armed Activities*, an argument gaining traction is that self-defence against non-State actors might be permitted if there was no real State governmental authority in the 'host' State, so attribution of the conduct to the State was not possible.[43] Known as the 'unwilling or unable' doctrine, a State may act in self-defence against a non-State group when the 'host' State is unwilling or unable to prevent those attacks.[44] Opinion is still divided on this question, and it is likely not yet accepted as a new rule of customary law.[45]

The second exception concerns the permissibility of using force for the purpose of the protection of nationals abroad. Some States have claimed a right to use force in the territory of another State, if the purpose of the force is

40 UNGA Res 2625 (XXV), Principle I; *Armed Activities*, para 161; UN Security Council, *Resolution 1373*, UN Doc S/RES/1373 (28 September 2011) (UNSC Res 1373), para 2; UNGA Res 3314 (XXIX).

41 UN Security Council, *Resolution 1368*, UN Doc S/RES/1368 (12 September 2001).

42 UNSC Res 1373.

43 *Armed Activities*, Separate Opinion of Judge Simma, para 11; Separate Opinion of Judge Kooijmans, paras 29–32.

44 Elena Chachko and Ashley Deeks, 'Which States Support the "Unwilling and Unable" Test?', *Lawfare* (10 October 2016), www.lawfareblog.com/which-states-support-unwilling-and-unable-test.

45 At a February 2021 informal Security Council meeting on 'the use of force in international law, non-State actors and legitimate self-defence', the right of self-defence against non-State actors was supported by seventeen States and rejected by four; the 'unwilling or unable' doctrine was supported by eight States and rejected by one: UN Security Council, *Letter Dated 8 March 2021 from the Permanent Representative of Mexico to the United Nations Addressed to the President of the Security Council*, UN Doc S/2021/247 (16 March 2021), annex I. See further Marc Schack, 'Resisting Clarity: Scandinavian Ambiguity in the "Unable or Unwilling" Debate' (2021) 90 *Nordic Journal of International Law* 31; Olivier Corten, 'The "Unwilling or Unable" Test: Has It Been, and Could It Be, Accepted?' (2016) 29 *Leiden Journal of International Law* 777; Ntina Tzouvala, 'The "Unwilling or Unable" Doctrine and the Political Economy of the War on Terror' (2023) 14 *Humanity* 19.

to protect their nationals from violence in the territorial State, most recently argued by Russia in its actions in Georgia[46] and Ukraine.[47] The arguments in support of such a claim are that it is a pre-existing customary right that was not extinguished by the adoption of the UN Charter; that it is not a use of force against the territorial integrity or political independence of the territorial State; and, finally, that it is a part of the right of self-defence as an attack directed against foreign nationals is, by extension, an attack on the State.[48] While persuasive, these arguments are not supported in practice and are unlikely to be considered customary international law.[49]

4.3 Relevance of the Law on the Use of Force to Nuclear Weapons and NC3

With this outline in mind, what then is the relevance for State NC3? While specific rules relating to NC3 and the use of force are detailed in the draft Code of Conduct in this study, it is useful at this stage to note some general principles. Clearly, there is a right for a State to use force to defend itself against an armed attack. The following questions then arise: Is it permissible for a State to have recourse to nuclear weapons to respond to an armed attack, regardless of whether that armed attack itself used nuclear weapons? Would that be a lawful, necessary, and proportionate act of self-defence?

It is necessary to review the only extant decision of the ICJ on the legality of the threat or use of nuclear weapons: the 1996 *Nuclear Weapons Advisory Opinion*, the result of a request from the General Assembly of the United Nations.[50] In phrasing its question to the ICJ, the Assembly drew on decades of its resolutions[51] condemning the use of nuclear weapons as a 'violation'

46 Independent International Fact-Finding Mission on the Conflict in Georgia, *Report* (2009), vol 1, para 23, www.mpil.de/en/pub/publications/archive/independent_international_fact.cfm.

47 See arguments put forward by Russia following the 2022 invasion of Ukraine – that it was acting to protect the ethnic Russian population in eastern Ukraine – and invoking Article 51: UN Security Council, Letter from the Permanent Representative of the Russian Federation to the United Nations Addressed to the Secretary-General, UN Doc S/2022/154 (24 February 2022).

48 See Natalino Ronzitti, 'Rescuing Nationals Abroad Revisited' (2019) 24 *Journal of Conflict and Security Law* 431.

49 Independent International Fact-Finding Mission on the Conflict in Georgia, *Report*, para 23.

50 UN General Assembly, *Resolution 49/75 K: Request for an Advisory Opinion from the International Court of Justice on the Legality of the Threat or Use of Nuclear Weapons*, UN Doc A/RES/49/75[K] (15 December 1994).

51 UN General Assembly, *Resolution 1653 (XVI)*, UN Doc A/RES/1653(XVI) (24 November 1961); *Resolution 33/71 B*, UN Doc A/RES/33/71[B] (14 December 1978); *Resolution 34/83 G*, UN Doc A/RES/34/83[G] (11 December 1979); *Resolution 35/152 D*, UN Doc A/RES/35/152[D] (12 December 1980); *Resolution 36/92 I*, UN Doc A/RES/36/92[I] (9 December 1981); *Resolution 45/59 B*, UN Doc A/RES/45/59[B] (4 December 1990); *Resolution 46/37 D*, UN Doc A/RES/46/37[D] (6 December 1991).

[of the UN Charter] and 'a crime against humanity'.[52] The question posed to the ICJ for consideration was this: 'Is the threat or use of nuclear weapons in any circumstance permitted under international law?'[53]

The Court subsequently made several relevant pronouncements on laws regarding the use of force. First, it noted that the prohibition on the use of force and the exceptions contained in the Charter (those of self-defence and collective action) applied to any use of force, 'regardless of the weapons employed', going on to note that the Charter 'neither expressly prohibits, nor permits, the use of any specific weapon, including nuclear weapons'.[54] The Court then held that, despite the fact that the use of nuclear weapons might breach other international law – specifically, the law of armed conflict[55] – it could not find that the threat or use of nuclear weapons was prohibited under international law. In particular, regarding the use of nuclear weapons in an action in self-defence, the Court stated that it could not 'conclude definitively whether the threat or use of nuclear weapons would be lawful or unlawful in an extreme circumstance of self-defence, in which the very survival of a State would be at stake'.[56] Likewise, the Court declined to state that the mere possession of nuclear weapons for the purposes of deterrence could be considered a threat of a use of force.[57]

The ICJ's Advisory Opinion is not binding. In any event, it was decided narrowly, on the question of the legality of using nuclear weapons in self-defence under the Charter, by seven votes to seven, with the president casting a vote in favour.[58] Were this decision to come before the Court today, it may well be that, in light of State practice since 1996, in particular in relation to the drafting and adoption of the TPNW[59] and the increasing role of international human rights law in times of armed conflict, the Court would decide differently. However, we can only speculate and must proceed within the framework of a decision that states that the use of nuclear weapons under the law on the use of force is not outright prohibited under customary law, or the UN Charter.

52 UN General Assembly, *Resolution 46/37 D: Convention on the Prohibition of the Use of Nuclear Weapons*, UN Doc A/RES/46/37[D] (6 December 1991), preamble.

53 *Nuclear Weapons Advisory Opinion*, para 1.

54 Para 39.

55 Para 42.

56 *Nuclear Weapons Advisory*.

57 See William H Boothby and Wolff Heintschel von Heinegg, *The Law on Nuclear Weapons: An International Commentary* (Edward Elgar, 2025), 80; Boothby and Heintschel von Heinegg, *Nuclear Weapons Law*, 190.

58 *Nuclear Weapons Advisory Opinion*, para 105.

59 Opened for signature 20 September 2017, entered into force 22 January 2021, 3379 UNTS 1 (TPNW).

In conclusion, the accepted position under international law remains that:

(a) simple possession of nuclear weapons does not amount to a threat of force or use of force; and
(b) under the law on the use of force, there is no customary prohibition on the use of nuclear weapons as part of a lawful response to an armed attack, but this is permissible only in extreme situations, such as a threat to the very existence of the State.

With this framework in mind, this study now examines the law on the conduct of hostilities to see what rules exist to govern the use of nuclear weapons during an armed conflict, such that they would require inclusion in State NC3.

5 The Law Relating to the Conduct of Hostilities

In addition to the law relating to the use of force, any NC3 framework would need to consider the international laws that govern the conduct of hostilities. If the decision is made to deploy nuclear weapons during an armed conflict, such deployment necessarily must be in accordance with the extant applicant treaty and international laws governing the conduct of hostilities. Failure to observe the laws of armed conflict while engaged in armed conflict may result in:

- a State being held responsible under the general law of State responsibility; and/or
- individual criminal sanction for perpetrators of breaches of international criminal law.

5.1 The Law of Armed Conflict

Known collectively as the law of armed conflict, the rules on the conduct of hostilities govern the permissible behaviour of parties to an armed conflict. There are over a dozen treaties that comprise the law of armed conflict, containing hundreds of provisions, as well as an expansive body of customary law.

Given that it is impossible for a study of this scope to closely examine *all* these treaties and provisions individually, this section will describe the overarching principles of the law most relevant for State NC3 systems.

The law of armed conflict has been broadly codified with the most relevant instruments for this study being:

- the Hague Conventions and Regulations of 1899 and 1907, including:
  - the 1899 Hague Convention (II) with Respect to the Laws and Customs of War on Land;[1]

1 Opened for signature 29 July 1899, entered into force 4 September 1900, 187 CTS 429.

DOI: 10.4324/9781003759294-5

  - the 1907 Hague Convention (IV) Respecting the Laws and Customs of War on Land and its annex, the Regulations Concerning the Laws and Customs of War on Land;[2]
  - the 1907 Hague Convention (V) Respecting the Rights and Duties of Neutral Powers and Persons in Case of War on Land;[3] and
  - the 1907 Hague Convention (XIII) Concerning the Rights and Duties of Neutral Powers in Naval War;[4]

- the 1949 Geneva Conventions[5] and 1977 Additional Protocols;[6] and
- the 1954 Hague Convention for the Protection of Cultural Property in the Event of Armed Conflict,[7]

as well as several weapons treaties that may have relevance for the use of nuclear weapons, in particular:

- the Convention on the Prohibition of Military or Any Other Hostile Use of Environmental Modification Techniques (ENMOD);[8]
- the Convention on the Prohibition of the Development, Production, and Stockpiling of Bacteriological (Biological) and Toxin Weapons and on Their Destruction (Biological Weapons Convention);[9] and

2 Opened for signature 18 October 1907, entered into force 26 January 1910, 205 CTS 277 and annex, Regulations Concerning the Laws and Customs of War on Land (Hague Regulations 1907).

3 Opened for signature 18 October 1907, entered into force 26 January 1910, 205 CTS 299.

4 Opened for signature 18 October 1907, entered into force 26 January 1910, 205 CTS 395.

5 Convention for the Amelioration of the Condition of the Wounded and Sick in Armed Forces in the Field, opened for signature 12 August 1949, entered into force 21 October 1950, 75 UNTS 31 (GCI); Convention for the Amelioration of the Condition of Wounded, Sick and Shipwrecked Members of Armed Forces at Sea, opened for signature 12 August 1949, entered into force 21 October 1950, 75 UNTS 85 (GCII); Convention relative to the Treatment of Prisoners of War, opened for signature 12 August 1949, entered into force 21 October 1950, 75 UNTS 135 (GCIII); Convention Relative to the Protection of Civilian Persons in Time of War, opened for signature 12 August 1949, entered into force 21 October 1950, 75 UNTS 287 (GCIV).

6 Protocol Additional to the Geneva Conventions of 12 August 1949, and Relating to the Protection of Victims of International Armed Conflicts, opened for signature 8 June 1977, entered into force 7 December 1978, 1125 UNTS 3 (API); Protocol Additional to the Geneva Conventions of 12 August 1949, and Relating to the Protection of Victims of Non-International Armed Conflicts, opened for signature 8 June 1977, entered into force 7 December 1978, 1125 UNTS 609 (APII).

7 Opened for signature 14 May 1954, entered into force 7 August 1956, 249 UNTS 240 (Hague Cultural Property Convention).

8 Opened for signature 10 December 1976, entered into force 5 October 1978, 1108 UNTS 151 (ENMOD).

9 Opened for signature 10 April 1972, entered into force 26 March 1975, 1015 UNTS 163 (Biological Weapons Convention).

- the Convention on the Prohibition of the Development, Production, Stockpiling, and Use of Chemical Weapons and on Their Destruction (Chemical Weapons Convention).[10]

Given that some States utilize sea-based and air-based nuclear weapons-launching platforms, the customary international law distinct to air and sea warfare should form a part of the NC3 of those nuclear States, in addition to the general law of armed conflict rules on the conduct of hostilities.

In a study of this size, it is difficult to summarize appropriately the rules of armed conflict without making some broad generalizations. For the most part, the rules can be largely reduced to two general, though not mutually exclusive, categories. One body of rules essentially aims to protect civilians and civilian objects during times of armed conflict. Broadly falling within this category are rules on occupied territory, rules protecting civilian persons detained in relation to the armed conflict, rules on the protection of items necessary for the survival of the civilian population, and prohibitions on targeting civilian objects or civilian persons (unless such persons are deemed as directly participating in the hostilities, or such objects can be considered military objectives due to their location, purpose, or use as military objectives).

The second body of law largely relates to protecting and governing persons who take a direct part in hostilities (such as combatants or any other persons who take a direct part in hostilities through, for instance, the use of a weapon or weapons system) or who otherwise accompany or assist those who take part in hostilities (such as medical personnel). This second body of law contains rules outlining permissible and impermissible acts for persons who take part in hostilities or who otherwise accompany such participants. This body of law includes rules on the protection of wounded, sick, and shipwrecked armed forces personnel on land and at sea; rules for the treatment of prisoners of war; prohibitions on the use of particular weapons in combat; and rules outlining what is considered a lawful target.

Within those two broad categories, it is possible to further discern certain principles that underpin nearly all the laws of armed conflict. These include:

- the principle of distinction and the prohibition on indiscriminate attacks, which anchor rules on the protection of civilians and civilian objects, as well as the law of targeting and the right of combatants to take a direct part in hostilities;
- the principle of military necessity, which underlies rules on targeting and permissible means and methods of warfare;
- the principle of proportionality, which is at the heart of rules on targeting;

10 Opened for signature 13 January 1993, entered into force 29 April 1997, 1974 UNTS 45 (Chemical Weapons Convention).

- the prohibition on causing unnecessary suffering and superfluous injury, which informs the existing weapons treaties and prohibitions on particular means and methods of warfare; and
- the principles of humanity and chivalry.

These principles are explored in more detail in the next section.

5.2 Note Regarding the Nuclear States and Additional Protocol I to the Geneva Conventions

Before going into detail regarding the foundational principles of the law of armed conflict, an important proviso must be outlined. Additional Protocol I (API)[11] codified several of the foundational principles of the law of armed conflict for the first time, including, inter alia, distinction and proportionality. However, some of the nuclear weapons States that became party to API took the position that these codifications – as they related to *weapons* specifically – were entirely new rules and therefore did not, in their opinion, apply to nuclear weapons.[12] Therefore, in the sections that follow, note will be made where specific codifications have been subject to reservations excluding their applicability to nuclear weapons.

5.3 General Principles of the Law of Armed Conflict

5.3.1 Distinction Between Combatants and Civilians

The principle of distinction is enunciated in Article 48 of API:

> In order to ensure respect for and protection of the civilian population and civilian objects, the Parties to the conflict shall at all times distinguish between the civilian population and combatants and between civilian objects and military objectives and accordingly shall direct their operations only against military objectives.

The principle is considered customary international law and has been acknowledged as one of the 'cardinal principles'[13] of international humanitarian law.

11 Opened for signature 8 June 1977, entered into force 7 December 1978, 1125 UNTS 3 (API).

12 William H Boothby, 'Law, Targeting and Nuclear Operations' (*NAPSNet Special Reports*, 31 October 2019), https://nautilus.org/napsnet/napsnet-special-reports/law-targeting-and-nuclear-operations/.

13 *Legality of the Threat or Use of Nuclear Weapons*, Advisory Opinion, 1996 ICJ Rep 226 (8 July) (*Nuclear Weapons Advisory Opinion*), para 78.

To observe the principle of distinction, parties to the armed conflict must at all times distinguish between civilians and combatants. Combatants are permitted to engage in hostilities,[14] and this lawful combat brings with it a customary international law immunity from prosecution for acts carried out during an armed conflict that are compliant with the law of armed conflict. However, combatants may also be targeted at any time during a conflict, by virtue of their status as combatants.[15] In the context of nuclear operations, combatants may be legally targeted under the law of armed conflict.

Civilians – all noncombatants[16] – must not be made the object of attack. However, if civilians can be deemed to be taking a direct part in hostilities (for example, because they are engaged in combat against a party to the conflict by use of a weapon or weapons system), they lose their immunity from targeting by virtue of that participation.[17] International law does not criminalize civilian participation in armed conflict, but neither does it immunize it.[18]

Therefore, to comply with the principle of distinction, any State NC3 should outline strict rules regarding who is authorized to take a direct part in nuclear hostilities. It should ensure that any civilians involved in nuclear operations are aware that they may be deemed as taking direct part in hostilities. Given the complexities of defining direct participation in hostilities,[19] any State NC3 should clearly outline what that State considers to be the threshold for direct participation in hostilities, both for its own personnel and for the purposes of targeting enemy personnel.

The principle of distinction also applies to objects. Attacks must only be directed against military objects and objectives; civilian objects must not be targeted.[20] A simple example would be that a military installation, such as an army base, would be lawfully targetable, while a prima facie civilian building, such as a religious installation (a church, mosque, or synagogue) or school, would not be lawfully targetable, unless said building was being used for military purposes and thereby became a military objective. Parties to an armed conflict must also observe the principle of distinction by ensuring that military and civilian persons and installations are clearly discernible as such; combatants must distinguish themselves from the civilian population through,

14 Under Hague Regulations 1907, art 1; API, art 43(2); GCIII, art 4A.

15 See generally Emily Crawford, *Identifying the Enemy: Civilian Participation in Armed Conflict* (Oxford University Press, 2015), 2–5.

16 API, art 50.

17 API, art 51(3).

18 Crawford, *Identifying the Enemy*, 3.

19 See Crawford, *Identifying the Enemy*, 48–91; ICRC, Customary IHL Database, Rule 6: Civilians' Loss of Protection from Attack, https://ihl-databases.icrc.org/en/customary-ihl/v1/rule6.

20 API, art 52.

for example, the use of uniforms or other visible insignia.[21] If there is doubt as to whether a person or object is civilian, the general presumption is that the person[22] or object[23] should be considered as civilian rather than military in nature and therefore not targetable.

The principle of distinction also underpins provisions which provide that persons who do not, or who no longer, take part in hostilities should not be targeted. The prohibition includes medical and religious personnel (along with any units, installations, and transports connected with such personnel),[24] as well as persons *hors de combat* (out of combat) due to illness, injury, shipwreck, or capture.[25]

5.3.2 Discrimination

Connected to the principle of distinction is the principle of discrimination – for example, there are rules designed to protect civilians by prohibiting attacks that employ indiscriminate weapons or tactics. Thus, Article 51(4) of API states that indiscriminate attacks are prohibited, with 'indiscriminate attacks' defined as attacks which are not directed at a specific military objective, which employ a means or method which cannot be directed at a specific military objective, or which employ a means or method the effects of which cannot be limited and are 'of a nature to strike military objectives and civilians or civilian objects without distinction'. Examples of an indiscriminate attack include one that is not aimed at a specific military target or that treats a number of distinct military targets as a single target (for example, carpet-bombing all the sites as if they were one target). Discrimination is thus a corollary of distinction, in that an attack that fails to observe the principle of distinction will likely be considered an indiscriminate attack. Any nuclear weapon that was indiscriminate in its effects would be captured by this prohibition; however, it should be noted that the indiscriminate attacks rule is considered by some nuclear weapons States (and nuclear umbrella States) as applying only to conventional weapons.[26]

21 See GCIII, art 4(A)(2)(b), relating to the requirement for combatants to wear a 'fixed distinctive sign recognizable at a distance'.

22 API, art 50(1).

23 API, art 52(3).

24 GCI, arts 19, 24, 25, 35, 36; GCII, arts 22, 24, 25, 27, 36–39, ch 4 generally; GCIII, art 33; GCIV, arts 18–22; API, arts 12, 15, 21–24, 26; APII, art 9.

25 See, for example, GCI, Common Article 3; GCII, art 12; GCIII, art 13; GCIV, art 27.

26 See statements on ratification by the United Kingdom (https://ihl-databases.icrc.org/en/ihl-treaties/api-1977/state-parties/gb?activeTab=undefined), France (https://ihl-databases.icrc.org/en/ihl-treaties/api-1977/state-parties/fr?activeTab=undefined), Canada (https://ihl-databases.icrc.org/en/ihl-treaties/api-1977/state-parties/ca?activeTab=undefined), and Germany (https://ihl-databases.icrc.org/en/ihl-treaties/api-1977/state-parties/de?activeTab=undefined).

5.3.3 Precautions in Attack

In undertaking targeting decisions, States must take precautions in attack to ensure that the civilian population, individual civilians, and civilian objects are spared as far as possible from the harmful effects of the armed conflict. The rules on precaution in attack are largely contained in Article 57 of API, which states that '[i]n the conduct of military operations, constant care shall be taken to spare the civilian population, civilians and civilian objects'.[27] Therefore:

2. With respect to attacks, the following precautions shall be taken:
   (a) those who plan or decide upon an attack shall:
      (i) do everything feasible to verify that the objectives to be attacked are neither civilians nor civilian objects and are not subject to special protection but are military objectives within the meaning of paragraph 2 of Article 52 and that it is not prohibited by the provisions of this Protocol to attack them;
      (ii) take all feasible precautions in the choice of means and methods of attack with a view to avoiding, and in any event to minimizing, incidental loss of civilian life, injury to civilians and damage to civilian objects;
      (iii) refrain from deciding to launch any attack which may be expected to cause incidental loss of civilian life, injury to civilians, damage to civilian objects, or a combination thereof, which would be excessive in relation to the concrete and direct military advantage anticipated;
   (b) an attack shall be cancelled or suspended if it becomes apparent that the objective is not a military one or is subject to special protection or that the attack may be expected to cause incidental loss of civilian life, injury to civilians, damage to civilian objects, or a combination thereof, which would be excessive in relation to the concrete and direct military advantage anticipated;
   (c) effective advance warning shall be given of attacks which may affect the civilian population, unless circumstances do not permit.
3. When a choice is possible between several military objectives for obtaining a similar military advantage, the objective to be selected shall be that the attack on which may be expected to cause the least danger to civilian lives and to civilian objects.

In the context of nuclear operations, the rules on precaution in attack require any State carrying out nuclear attacks to ensure observance of the constant

27 API, art 57(1).

care provision,[28] the requirement to verify target status,[29] limitations on choice of means or methods,[30] limitations on possible targets,[31] the requirement to give warnings where feasible,[32] and the obligation to cancel or suspend attacks if a breach of distinction or proportionality seems likely.[33] Additionally, States are under an obligation to take precautions in defence and to limit the effects of attacks directed against themselves,[34] such as removing civilian populations from the vicinity of military objectives and avoiding locating military objectives in civilian populated areas.[35] However, it should be noted that the obligations in defence are not absolute – they are only to be undertaken to the 'maximum extent feasible'.

Additionally, there are certain installations and objects that require special consideration in targeting, if targeting such installations or objects would result in serious adverse consequences for the civilian population. This principle underpins rules regarding targeting works containing dangerous forces (such as dams, dykes, and nuclear electrical generating stations)[36] and objects indispensable for the survival of the civilian population (such as water supplies and foodstuffs).[37] It is likewise prohibited to target cultural property, unless military necessity imperatively requires such targeting.[38]

These precautionary measures (in both attack and defence) must be taken in addition to observing rules on distinction and proportionality. They could include such measures as instructing the population regarding access to fallout shelters, carrying out evacuation drills, providing protective equipment and supplies, and establishing warning systems for impending attacks.[39] It should be noted that for certain nuclear and nuclear umbrella States, Article 57(2)–(3) introduced new rules which, in the opinion of those States, do not apply to nuclear weapons.[40]

28 API, art 57(1).
29 API, art 57(2)(a)(i).
30 API, art 57(2)(a)(ii).
31 API, art 57(3).
32 Hague Regulations 1907, art 26; API, art 57(2)(c).
33 API, art 57(2)(b).
34 API, art 58(c).
35 API, art 58(b). See also API, art 51(7).
36 API, art 56; APII, art 15.
37 API, art 54(2).
38 Hague Regulations 1907, art 27; Convention (IX) Concerning Bombardment by Naval Forces in Time of War, opened for signature 18 October 1907, entered into force 26 January 1910, 205 CTS 345, art 5; API, art 53; APII, art 16; Hague Cultural Property Convention, art 4.
39 See civil defence procedures in States such as South Korea and Japan, which routinely instruct their civilian populations on shelter and evacuation procedures: Hyonhee Shin and Ju-min Park, 'South Korea Holds Rare Air Raid Drill, But Many Citizens Ignore It', *Reuters* (23 August 2023), www.reuters.com/world/asia-pacific/south-korea-hold-first-nationwide-defence-drills-6-years-amid-north-threats-2023-08-23/.
40 See statements on ratification by Italy (https://ihl-databases.icrc.org/en/ihl-treaties/api-1977/state-parties/it?activeTab=undefined), the Netherlands (https://ihl-databases.icrc.org/en/ihl-treaties/

5.3.4 Military Necessity

Military necessity requires parties to the conflict adopt *only* those measures necessary to weaken the enemy and achieve their surrender – not to bring about total destruction of the enemy, its armed forces, or its property. As elaborated in *United States v List*, a war crimes case from the Second World War:

> Military necessity permits a belligerent, subject to the laws of war, to apply any amount and kind of force to compel the complete submission of the enemy with the least possible expenditure of time, life, and money. In general, it . . . permits the destruction of life of armed enemies and other persons whose destruction is incidentally unavoidable by the armed conflicts of the war . . . but it does not permit the killing of innocent inhabitants for purposes of revenge or the satisfaction of a lust to kill. The destruction of property to be lawful must be imperatively demanded by the necessities of war. Destruction as an end in itself is a violation of international law. There must be some reasonable connection between the destruction of property and the overcoming of the enemy forces.[41]

Although the principle of military necessity is not outlined in either the Geneva Conventions or the Additional Protocols, the essence of the principle finds expression in the rule on proportionality. The concept of military necessity is found in the 1907 Hague Regulations[42] and the Rome Statute of the International Criminal Court (ICC).[43]

5.3.5 Proportionality

The principle of proportionality requires that any military measures taken by parties to the conflict must be proportionate. As outlined in API, Article 51(5)(b) defines a disproportionate attack as 'an attack which may be expected to cause incidental loss of civilian life, injury to civilians, damage to civilian objects, or a combination thereof, which would be excessive in relation to the concrete and direct military advantage anticipated'. However, it must be noted that not just any loss of civilian life renders an attack disproportionate.

---

api-1977/state-parties/nl?activeTab=undefined), and Spain (https://ihl-databases.icrc.org/en/ihl-treaties/api-1977/state-parties/es?activeTab=undefined).

41 *United States v List (Hostage Case)*, 11 *Trials of War Criminals Before the Nuremberg Military Tribunals under Control Council Law No. 10*, at 1253–1254.

42 Hague Regulations 1907, art 23(g).

43 Rome Statute of the International Criminal Court, opened for signature 17 July 1998, entered into force 1 July 2002, 2187 UNTS 90 (Rome Statute). Article 8(2)(b)(xiii) of the Rome Statute provides that the destruction or seizure of enemy property when not 'imperatively demanded by the necessities of war' constitutes a war crime.

The key term in Article 51(5)(b) is 'incidental'. Therefore, the principle of proportionality will only be violated if the 'collateral civilian casualties would be disproportionate to the specific military gain from the attack'.[44]

5.3.6 Limitation on Means and Methods of Warfare

One of the fundamental principles of the law of armed conflict is that the choice of means and methods available to parties to the conflict is not unlimited.[45] Therefore, certain types of attack and certain types of weapons are either strictly limited or outright prohibited. In terms of limitations on methods of warfare that would be relevant for nuclear operations, there are prohibitions on violence (or threats of violence) if the primary purpose is to spread terror among the civilian population[46] – a threatened nuclear attack done solely or primarily for the purpose of causing terror would run afoul of this prohibition.

Perfidy – defined as '[a]cts inviting the confidence of an adversary to lead him to believe that he is entitled to, or is obliged to accord, protection under the rules of international law applicable in armed conflict, with intent to betray that confidence' – is also forbidden.[47] This rule would be breached if, as Boothby and Heintschel von Heinegg note, a nuclear attack were launched from an aircraft bearing civilian markings that was feigning civilian status (and thus prima facie immune from being attacked by the adverse party).[48] Intentional misuse of protected or distinctive emblems and signs – for example, the emblems of the Red Cross[49] or the United Nations,[50] flags of truce,[51] or neutral[52] or enemy[53] indicators – is likewise a prohibited method of war under the law of armed conflict.

Finally, it is prohibited to engage in reprisals against certain protected persons and objects. A reprisal is an act which prima facie violates the law of armed conflict, but which, when done in response to a prior violation of the law of armed conflict by another State, is rendered lawful. Reprisals are generally permissible under the law of armed conflict but may not be carried out against certain categories of persons or objects, including the wounded, sick,

44 *Nuclear Weapons Advisory Opinion*, Dissenting Opinion of Judge Higgins, 587.
45 Hague Regulations 1907, art 22; API, art 35(1).
46 API, art 51(2); APII, art 13(2).
47 API, art 37(1); Rome Statute, art 8(2)(b)(xi).
48 See further William H Boothby and Wolff Heintschel von Heinegg, *The Law on Nuclear Weapons: An International Commentary* (Edward Elgar, 2025), 192.
49 GCI, arts 38–44; GCII, arts 41–45.
50 API, art 38(2).
51 Hague Regulations 1907, art 23(f); API, art 38(1).
52 API, art 39(1).
53 Hague Regulations 1907, art 23(f); API, art 39(2).

and shipwrecked; medical personnel and chaplains; medical units, establishments, and transports; prisoners of war; and protected persons (such as civilians) and their property.[54] However, some nuclear or nuclear umbrella States, including France and the United Kingdom, have reserved the right to resort to reprisals that might be contrary to API.[55]

5.3.7 Prohibition on Causing Unnecessary Suffering and Superfluous Injury

The international law of armed conflict also prohibits the use of means and methods of warfare which cause unnecessary suffering or superfluous injury. This principle is at the core of many of the weapons treaties that exist in the law of armed conflict and prohibits causing injuries against combatants that are greater than what is strictly necessary to achieve legitimate military objectives or that uselessly aggravate the suffering of wounded personnel without increasing the military advantage gained by the use of the weapon.[56] The prohibition is contained in the 1907 Hague Regulations[57] and in API[58] and is at the core of the 1980 Convention on Prohibitions or Restrictions on the Use of Certain Conventional Weapons Which May Be Deemed to Be Excessively Injurious or to Have Indiscriminate Effects.[59]

Beyond the nuclear weapons–specific treaties, such as the TPNW[60] (discussed further later in this chapter), it is necessary to make specific note of the Chemical Weapons Convention and the Biological Weapons Convention. Nuclear weapons are not chemical or biological weapons;[61] however, the published nuclear doctrine of certain States, such as Russia, specifies that nuclear weapons would be used in response to an attack with WMDs, such as chemical and biological weapons.

54 For reprisals prohibited under the Geneva Conventions, see GCI, art 14; GCII, art 16; GCIII, art 13; GCIV, art 33.

55 See the rule on permissible and impermissible reprisals: ICRC, Customary IHL Database, Rule 145: Reprisals. For the question of nuclear reprisals, see Scott Sagan and Allen Weiner, 'The Illegality of Targeting Civilians by Way of Belligerent Reprisal: Implications for U.S. Nuclear Doctrine', *Just Security* (10 May 2021).

56 Gary D Solis, *The Law of Armed Conflict: International Humanitarian Law in War* (3rd ed, Cambridge University Press, 2022), 226.

57 Hague Regulations 1907, art 23.

58 API, art 36, noting that API uses slightly different wording, prohibiting weapons 'of a nature' to cause unnecessary suffering.

59 Entered into force 2 December 1983, 1342 UNTS 137.

60 Treaty on the Prohibition of Nuclear Weapons, opened for signature 20 September 2017, entered into force 22 January 2021, 3379 UNTS 1 (TPNW).

61 On whether nuclear weapons can be considered poison weapons, see further Boothby and Heintschel von Heinegg, *The Law on Nuclear Weapons*, 277–278.

5.3.8 Humanity, Chivalry, and the Martens Clause

Finally, note should be made regarding a principle that finds inclusion in the military manuals of some States[62] – the idea that States are bound in their conduct to observe the principle of 'humanity' or 'chivalry'.[63] State practice has furnished definitions of 'humanity' and 'chivalry' that seem largely similar to the doctrines of military necessity and the principle of proportionality[64] or else a rewording of the prohibition on causing unnecessary suffering or superfluous injury.[65] Therefore, humanity and chivalry would not seem to be distinct legal principles in the same way as distinction, but rather convenient descriptors for other doctrines and principles such as proportionality.

If humanity is not a distinct principle in the law, then why mention it? Simply put, it is necessary to mention humanity because of the origins of the concept in times of armed conflict, which can be traced back to the so-called Martens Clause. First included in the law of armed conflict in the Hague Regulations,[66] the Clause was acknowledged by the ICJ in the *Nuclear Weapons Advisory Opinion* as an important foundational principle of the law of armed conflict.[67] Indeed, it is also found in the preamble to the TPNW. Therefore, any discussion of the use or possession of nuclear weapons would need to note the Martens Clause, which states:

> Until a more complete code of the laws of war is issued, the High Contracting Parties think it right to declare that in cases not included in the Regulations adopted by them, populations and belligerents remain under the protection and empire of the principles of international law, as they result from the usages established between civilized nations, from the laws of humanity and the requirements of the public conscience.[68]

62 Including UK Ministry of Defence, *The Joint Service Manual of the Law of Armed Conflict* (JSP 383, 2004) (UK LOAC Manual), para 2.4; US Department of Defense, *Law of War Manual* (June 2015, updated July 2023) (US DoD Law of War Manual), § 2.3; Canada, *Joint Doctrine Manual: Law of Armed Conflict at the Operational and Tactical Levels* (B-GJ-005-104/FP-021, 2001), para 202(6) (Canada LOAC Manual).

63 Canada LOAC Manual, para 202(7).

64 The UK LOAC Manual defines humanity as a rule that 'forbids the infliction of suffering, injury, or destruction not actually necessary for the accomplishment of legitimate military purposes': para 2.4.

65 The US DoD Law of War Manual states '*[h]umanity* may be defined as the principle that forbids the infliction of suffering, injury, or destruction unnecessary to accomplish a legitimate military purpose': § 2.3.

66 Hague Regulations 1907, preamble.

67 See further *Nuclear Weapons Advisory Opinion*, para 87.

68 See Jean Pictet (ed), *Commentary to the Third Geneva Convention Relative to the Treatment of Prisoners of War* (ICRC, 1960), 46–47.

While it is still debatable what the Clause actually provides for,[69] it would seem, at a minimum, that any decision to use nuclear weapons would have to ensure that such use was not contrary to the extant treaty or customary international law, particularly the principles of the law of armed conflict.

5.4 Nuclear Weapons and the Natural Environment in Armed Conflict

In the context of rules guiding the use of nuclear weapons, the natural environment must also be considered. There are some limited rules that relate to the natural environment, either providing for its protection from deliberate targeting (if such targeting were to result in excessive and long-term damage) or else prohibiting weaponizing the natural environment through manipulation of natural environmental forces.

In the first category – rules designed to limit the targeting of the natural environment – Article 35(3) of API provides that '[i]t is prohibited to employ methods or means of warfare which are intended, or may be expected, to cause widespread, long-term and severe damage to the natural environment'. This is reaffirmed in Article 55 of API, which states:

> Care shall be taken in warfare to protect the natural environment against widespread, long-term and severe damage. This protection includes a prohibition of the use of methods or means of warfare which are intended or may be expected to cause such damage to the natural environment and thereby to prejudice the health or survival of the population.

In the specific context of nuclear weapons, the importance of protecting the natural environment was affirmed by the ICJ in the *Nuclear Weapons Advisory Opinion*, where the Court stated that 'the environment is not an abstraction but represents the living space, the quality of life and the very health of human beings, including generations unborn'.[70] The International Committee of the Red Cross (ICRC) asserts that the rules on the protection of the natural environment are considered customary international law, in international and, probably, non-international armed conflicts (notwithstanding the law of non-international armed conflict containing no specific provision

69 See Mitchell Stapleton-Coory, 'The Enduring Legacy of the Martens Clause: Resolving the Conflict of Morality in International Humanitarian Law' (2019) 40 *Adelaide Law Review* 471; Antonio Cassese, 'The Martens Clause: Half a Loaf or Simply Pie in the Sky?' (2000) 11 *European Journal of International Law* 187, 193–198; Vitaliy Ivanenko, 'The Origins, Causes and Enduring Significance of the Martens Clause: A View from Russia' (2022) 104 *International Review of the Red Cross* 1708.

70 *Nuclear Weapons Advisory Opinion*, para 29.

regarding the protection of the natural environment),[71] with more recent State practice suggesting that the requirement to protect the natural environment in armed conflict is increasingly viewed as customary in both international and non-international armed conflict.[72] Therefore, any decision that leads to the use of nuclear weapons would have to consider the applicable rules on the protection of the natural environment.

In the second category – rules limiting the manipulation of the natural environment – note should be made of the 1976 ENMOD, which prohibits the use of environmental modification techniques as weapons of warfare. The term 'environmental modification techniques' is defined in Article II as 'any technique for changing – through the deliberate manipulation of natural processes – the dynamics, composition or structure of the Earth, including its biota, lithosphere, hydrosphere and atmosphere, or of outer space'. Examples include creating earthquakes and tsunamis, as well as changing weather patterns, ocean currents, the ozone layer, and the ionosphere.[73]

ENMOD provides that States parties shall not engage in 'military or any other hostile use of environmental modification techniques having widespread, long-lasting or severe effects as the means of destruction, damage or injury to any other State Party'.[74] The Convention thus prohibits manipulation of the natural environment for use as a weapon of war and 'prohibits direct and intentional destruction of any element of the environment with the explicit purpose of using that destruction as a way of causing destruction, damage, or injury to another State that is a party to the treaty'.[75] As with the rules on the protection of the environment, any State party to ENMOD would have to ensure that it did not use nuclear weapons in such a way as to modify the environment for hostile purpose such that the modification and manipulation of the environment themselves became a weapon of war.

The next chapter of this book turns to look at how international criminal law applies to nuclear operations and would have to be considered in any robust NC3 system.

71 See ICRC, Customary IHL Database, Rules 43–45, https://ihl-databases.icrc.org/en/customary-ihl/v1.

72 See International Law Commission, *Report of the International Law Commission on the Work of Its Seventy-third Session (18 April–3 June and 4 July–5 August 2022)*, UN Doc A/77/10 (2022), commentary to Principle 13, para 6, which notes that there is still divided opinion on the customary status of the protection of the environment in international armed conflict and non-international armed conflict, under API and APII.

73 United Nations, *Report of the Conference of the Committee on Disarmament: Volume I*, General Assembly, Official Records, Thirty-first Session, Supplement No 27, UN Doc A/31/27 (1976), 92, https://digitallibrary.un.org/record/697097.

74 ENMOD, art I(1).

75 William Boothby, *The Law of Targeting* (Oxford University Press, 2012), 201.

6 International Criminal Law

As previously noted, there is no universally applicable prohibition on the use of nuclear weapons, notwithstanding the existence of the TPNW.[1] That being said, any NC3 infrastructure must consider that any decision to use a nuclear weapon *may* trigger the application of international criminal law – in particular, if the use of nuclear weapons can be classified as (a) a genocidal act or a crime against humanity (neither of which requires the existence of an armed conflict) or (b) a war crime (which does require the existence of an armed conflict). Therefore, any State NC3 would need to ensure that operators involved in nuclear launch decision-making are aware of the relevant aspects of international criminal law and possible international criminal culpability.

Because the Rome Statute of the International Criminal Court[2] is the most recent iteration of international criminal law in treaty form, it will serve as the basis for the analysis in this chapter. Because the Statute was intended by the drafters of the ICC to largely reflect the customary international criminal law of the time, we will dedicate due attention to the formulations of the relevant crimes in the Statute.[3] In order to understand what amounts to a criminal act under the Statute, recourse must also be had to the ICC's Elements of Crimes, which were adopted to assist the Court in the interpretation and application of the crime provisions of the Statute.[4] To understand the scope and meaning

1 Treaty on the Prohibition of Nuclear Weapons, opened for signature 20 September 2017, entered into force 22 January 2021, 3379 UNTS 1 (TPNW).

2 Opened for signature 17 July 1998, entered into force 1 July 2002, 2187 UNTS 90 (Rome Statute).

3 See Leila Nadya Sadat, *The International Criminal Court and the Transformation of International Law: Justice for the New Millenium* (Brill, 2002), 261–274; Christine Byron, *War Crimes and Crimes against Humanity in the Rome Statute of the International Criminal Court* (Manchester University Press, 2009), 4; Robert Cryer, Håkan Friman, Darryl Robinson, and Elizabeth Wilmshurst, *An Introduction to International Criminal Law and Procedure* (3rd ed, Cambridge University Press, 2014), 151.

4 The Elements of Crimes are reproduced from the *Official Records of the Assembly of States Parties to the Rome Statute of the International Criminal Court, First Session, New York, 3–10 September 2002* (United Nations, Sales No E.03.V.2 and corrigendum), pt II.B. The Elements of Crimes adopted at the 2010 Review Conference are replicated from the *Official Records of the*

DOI: 10.4324/9781003759294-6

of a particular crime and its commission, in particular in relation to the use of nuclear weapons, examining the relevant Elements of Crime is essential.

Not all States in the world are party to the Rome Statute of the International Criminal Court, and, of the nuclear weapons States, only two (France and the United Kingdom) have ratified the ICC Statute.

For France, it is the State's position that:

> The provisions of article 8 of the Statute, in particular paragraph 2 (b) thereof, relate solely to conventional weapons and can neither regulate nor prohibit the possible use of nuclear weapons nor impair the other rules of international law applicable to other weapons necessary to the exercise by France of its inherent right of self-defence, unless nuclear weapons or the other weapons referred to herein become subject in the future to a comprehensive ban and are specified in an annex to the Statute by means of an amendment adopted in accordance with the provisions of articles 121 and 123.[5]

The United Kingdom's ratification statement referred to API[6] and nuclear weapons:

> The United Kingdom understands the term 'the established framework of international law', used in article 8 (2) (b) and (e), to include customary international law as established by State practice and *opinio juris*. In that context the United Kingdom confirms and draws to the attention of the Court its views as expressed, inter alia, in its statements made on ratification of relevant instruments of international law, including the Protocol Additional to the Geneva Conventions of 12th August 1949, and relating to the Protection of Victims of International Armed Conflicts (Protocol I) of 8th June 1977.[7]

Therefore, any consideration of nuclear weapons and international criminal law under the ICC would, for France and the United Kingdom, need to be understood in light of these statements.

Review Conference of the Rome Statute of the International Criminal Court, Kampala, 31 May – 11 June 2010 (International Criminal Court, RC/11, 2010).

5 Interpretative declaration made by France on ratification of the Rome Statute on 9 June 2000, para 2: UN Treaty Collection, 'Rome Statute of the International Criminal Court', https://treaties.un.org/pages/ViewDetails.aspx?src=TREATY&mtdsg_no=XVIII-10&chapter=18&clang=_en.

6 Protocol Additional to the Geneva Conventions of 12 August 1949, and Relating to the Protection of Victims of International Armed Conflicts, opened for signature 8 June 1977, entered into force 7 December 1978, 1125 UNTS 3 (API).

7 Declaration made by the United Kingdom on ratification of the Rome Statute on 4 October 2001, UN Treaty Collection, 'Rome Statute of the International Criminal Court', https://treaties.un.org/pages/ViewDetails.aspx?src=TREATY&mtdsg_no=XVIII-10&chapter=18&clang=_en.

6.1 Genocide

The use of a nuclear weapon might, in certain instances, amount to an act of genocide,[8] defined in Article 6 of the Rome Statute:

> 'genocide' means any of the following acts committed with intent to destroy, in whole or in part, a national, ethnical, racial or religious group, as such:
>
> (a) Killing members of the group;
> (b) Causing serious bodily or mental harm to members of the group;
> (c) Deliberately inflicting on the group conditions of life calculated to bring about its physical destruction in whole or in part;
> (d) Imposing measures intended to prevent births within the group;
> (e) Forcibly transferring children of the group to another group.

Article 6 of the Rome Statute reproduces the text of Article II of the 1948 Genocide Convention and is considered customary international law.[9] There is no requirement for a pre-existing armed conflict to be underway for the crime of genocide to be recognized. The use of a nuclear weapon, even in the execution of an act of self-defence, could therefore be a genocidal act if the relevant elements of crime are made out.

Of the five possible ways in which genocide may be committed, the most relevant to nuclear weapons are killing or causing serious bodily harm to members of a group (conditions 6a and 6b, respectively).

According to the Elements of Crimes, the threshold for 6(a) will be met if:

1. The perpetrator killed one or more persons.
2. Such person or persons belonged to a particular national, ethnical, racial, or religious group.
3. The perpetrator intended to destroy, in whole or in part, that national, ethnical, racial, or religious group, as such.
4. The conduct took place in the context of a manifest pattern of similar conduct directed against that group or was conduct that could itself effect such destruction.[10]

8 Genocide is prohibited and designated a crime in the Genocide Convention (opened for signature 9 December 1948, entered into force 12 January 1951, 78 UNTS 276.) For the purposes of this section, attention is focused solely on the individual criminal aspects of genocide (as well as individual criminal responsibility for crimes against humanity and war crimes), rather than questions of State responsibility.

9 See *Application of the Convention on the Prevention and Punishment of the Crime of Genocide (Bosnia and Herzegovina v Serbia and Montenegro)*, Judgment, 2007 ICJ Rep 43 (26 February) (*Bosnian Genocide*), para 161.

10 Elements of Crimes, art 6(a).

Therefore, the use of a nuclear weapon could be deemed genocide by killing if:

- the nuclear weapon was aimed at, and did in fact kill, one or more persons of a specific national, racial, ethnical, or religious group;
- the attacker intended to destroy that group, either in whole or in part; and
- the attack was part of a clear pattern or similar behaviour already directed at the group in question, or the attack on its own was able to achieve the outcome of the destruction of the group in whole or in part.

The 'in part' referred to in the Elements of Crimes has been interpreted, in practice, to mean a substantial part of the specific group – such as a significant numerical percentage of the group, a substantial part of the group located in a particular geographical area, or a substantial part of the group that serves a particular function regarding the group as a whole – that is, if such persons targeted in a genocidal attack were community leaders.[11] Additionally, the attack must be connected with a clear pattern of similar behaviour directed at the group (for example, a series of attacks targeting them). A single attack could also meet the threshold, so long as it had the capability of destroying, in whole or in part, the group in question. Therefore, a series of small-scale nuclear attacks against a specific group or a single large nuclear attack against a group could amount to a genocidal act if it met this threshold.

For causing serious bodily or mental harm to members of the group, the required elements are:

1. The perpetrator caused serious bodily or mental harm to one or more persons.[12]
2. Such person or persons belonged to a particular national, ethnical, racial, or religious group.
3. The perpetrator intended to destroy, in whole or in part, that national, ethnical, racial, or religious group, as such.
4. The conduct took place in the context of a manifest pattern of similar conduct directed against that group or was conduct that could itself effect such destruction.[13]

11 *Prosecutor v Radislav Krstić*, Case No IT-98–33-A, Appeals Chamber Judgment (ICTY, 19 April 2004), para 15; *Prosecutor v Radoslav Brđanin*, Case No IT-99–36-T, Judgment (ICTY, 1 September 2004), para 702; *Prosecutor v Clément Kayishema and Obed Ruzindana*, Case No ICTR-95–1-T, Judgment (International Criminal Tribunal for Rwanda, 21 May 1999), para 97; *Case 002/02*, Case File No 002/19-09-2007/ECCC/TC, Judgment (Extraordinary Chambers in the Courts of Cambodia, 16 November 2018), para 802; *Prosecutor v Omar Hassan Ahmad Al Bashir*, Pre-trial Chamber I, ICC-02/05-01/09, Decision on the Prosecution's Application for a Warrant of Arrest against Omar Hassan Ahmad Al Bashir (4 March 2009), Separate and Partly Dissenting Opinion of Judge Anita Ušacka, para 67; *Bosnian Genocide*, paras 198–200.

12 A footnote indicates that '[t]his conduct may include, but is not necessarily restricted to, acts of torture, rape, sexual violence or inhuman or degrading treatment'. Such activities, when combined with certain nuclear-related operations, such as of the kind mentioned in the discussion of this offence, might, if taken together, amount to this form of genocide.

13 Elements of Crimes, art 6(b).

Elements 2–4 of the crime of causing serious bodily or mental harm are identical to elements 2–4 of genocidal killing, so reference should be made to the previous discussion. For the elements of causing serious bodily or mental harm, an example of such an attack would include any attack that causes serious physical illness through, for example, injury through radiation, blast, fire, or fragmentation damage as a result of the use of a nuclear weapon, provided the additional elements 2–4 are also found.

In the context of a nuclear attack, and for the purposes of an NC3 code of conduct, a series of nuclear attacks or a single large-scale nuclear attack could amount to an act of genocide, provided the elements of a genocidal act were made out. Therefore, any State NC3 should ensure that any personnel engaged in nuclear operations are instructed in the law regarding genocide and when their participation in nuclear operations might amount to such a crime.

6.2 Crimes Against Humanity

In the absence of long-debated treaties on crimes against humanity,[14] the Rome Statute again provides the most recent legal framework. Under this Statute, crimes against humanity are any of a number of acts 'when committed as part of a widespread or systematic attack directed against any civilian population, with knowledge of the attack'.[15] For the purposes of a code on NC3, the most relevant act would seem to be the crime against humanity of murder, outlined in Article 7(1)(a).

Determining the existence of a crime against humanity requires analysis of the constituent elements: that the attack was directed against the civilian population; that the attack was carried out in pursuance of a policy of a State or organization; that the attack was widespread or systematic; that the attack was connected to that organizational policy; and that the perpetrator of the attack knew that the conduct was part of, or intended the conduct to be part of, a widespread or systematic attack directed against a civilian population.[16]

Additionally, reference must be made to Article 7(2)(a), which provides that an '[a]ttack directed against any civilian population' means 'a course of conduct involving the multiple commission of [the listed acts] against any civilian population, pursuant to or in furtherance of a State or organizational policy to commit such attack'.[17]

14 See International Law Commission, 'Analytical Guide to the Work of the International Law Commission: Crimes Against Humanity', https://legal.un.org/ilc/guide/7_7.shtml.

15 Rome Statute, art 7(1).

16 *Prosecutor v Germain Katanga*, Trial Chamber II, ICC-01/04-01/07, Judgment pursuant to Article 74 of the Statute (7 March 2014), paras 1097–1099.

17 Rome Statute, art 7(2)(a).

The elements of the crime against humanity of murder are that:

1. The perpetrator killed one or more persons.
2. The conduct was committed as part of a widespread or systematic attack directed against a civilian population.
3. The perpetrator knew that the conduct was part of or intended the conduct to be part of a widespread or systematic attack against a civilian population.[18]

Therefore, for the elements of crime against humanity of murder to be met, the perpetrator must have killed one or more persons as part of a widespread and systematic attack. The word 'widespread' is to be understood as 'massive, frequent, carried out collectively with considerable seriousness and directed against a multiplicity of victims',[19] encompassing either a series of acts that have a cumulative effect or acts that, collectively, have the singular impact of 'an inhumane act of extraordinary magnitude'.[20] The word 'systematic' refers to the 'organised nature of the acts of violence and the improbability of their random occurrence'.[21] In this respect, 'systematic' is also intended to refer to the existence of an organizational policy (whether of a State or a non-State group). Finally, the perpetrator must know that the attack forms part of that policy, although the prosecution does not need specifically to prove that the perpetrator had knowledge of all characteristics of the attack or the precise details of the plan or policy of the State or organization.

In the context of a nuclear attack, and for the purposes of an NC3 code of conduct, a series of nuclear attacks or a single large-scale nuclear attack could amount to a crime against humanity, provided such attack killed one or more persons, was committed as part of other widespread and systematic attacks, and was directed against the civilian population with knowledge that the attack was being conducted in such a manner, pursuant to a State or organizational policy. Therefore, any State NC3 should ensure that any personnel engaged in nuclear operations are instructed in the law regarding crimes against humanity and when their participation in nuclear operations might amount to such a crime.

18 Elements of Crimes, art 7(1)(a).

19 *Prosecutor v Jean-Pierre Bemba Gombo*, Pre-Trial Chamber II, ICC-01/05-01/08, Decision Pursuant to Article 61(7)(a) and (b) of the Rome Statute on the Charges of the Prosecutor against Jean-Pierre Bemba Gombo (15 June 2009), para 83.

20 See, for example, *Prosecutor v Vidoje Blagojević and Dragan Jokić*, Case No IT-02-60-T, Trial Chamber I, Section A Judgment (ICTY, 17 January 2005), para 545.

21 *Prosecutor v Germain Katanga*, Pre-Trial Chamber I, ICC-01/04-01/07, Decision on the evidence and information provided by the Prosecution for the issuance of a warrant of arrest against Germain Katanga (6 July 2007), para 33.

6.3 War Crimes

Arguably the most relevant laws on war crimes are those that relate to civilians – specifically, deliberate attacks against civilians and civilian objects and the launch of attacks that cause excessive incidental death, injury, or damage to civilians and civilian objects. Boothby and Heintschel von Heinegg also suggest that the prohibition on the use of poison weapons could be relevant if nuclear weapons can be categorized as such[22] – this would depend on categorizing one of the deleterious effects of a nuclear weapon as being a form of poison.

To establish a case for war crimes, there needs to be a pre-existing armed conflict (either international or non-international). There is copious literature regarding how to define an international and a non-international armed conflict.[23] For the purposes of this chapter, we will reference the accepted definition outlined by the International Criminal Tribunal for the former Yugoslavia (ICTY) in the *Tadić* case: that an armed conflict exists 'whenever there is a resort to armed force between States or protracted armed violence between governmental authorities and organized armed groups or between such groups within a State'.[24]

6.3.1 Attacking Civilians and Civilian Objects

A deliberate attack against civilians and/or civilian objects using a nuclear weapon would amount to a war crime under Article 8(2)(b)(i) of the Rome Statute, which criminalizes '[i]ntentionally directing attacks against the civilian population as such or against individual civilians not taking direct part in hostilities', when carried out in the context of an international armed conflict. The elements of this crime are:

1. The perpetrator directed an attack.
2. The object of the attack was a civilian population as such or individual civilians not taking direct part in hostilities.

22 William H Boothby and Wolff Heintschel von Heinegg, *The Law on Nuclear Weapons: An International Commentary* (Edward Elgar, 2025), 277–278.

23 See Anthony Cullen, *The Concept of Non-International Armed Conflict in International Humanitarian Law* (Cambridge University Press, 2010); Mary Ellen O'Connell, 'Defining Armed Conflict' (2008) 13 *Journal of Conflict and Security Law* 393; Stuart Casey-Maslen and Steven Haines, 'Defining an Armed Conflict', in *Hague Law Interpreted* (Bloomsbury Publishing, 2018); Rogier Bartels, 'The Classification of Armed Conflicts by International Criminal Courts and Tribunals' (2020) 20 *International Criminal Law Review* 595; Noam Zamir, 'The Distinction Between International and Non-International Armed Conflicts', in *Classification of Conflicts in International Humanitarian Law: The Legal Impact of Foreign Intervention in Civil Wars* (Edward Elgar, 2017).

24 *Prosecutor v Dusko Tadić*, Case No IT-94-1-AR72, Appeals Chamber, Decision (ICTY, 2 October 1995), para 70.

3. The perpetrator intended the civilian population as such or individual civilians not taking direct part in hostilities to be the object of the attack.
4. The conduct took place in the context of and was associated with an international armed conflict.
5. The perpetrator was aware of factual circumstances that established the existence of an armed conflict.[25]

Article 8(2)(b)(ii) criminalizes '[i]ntentionally directing attacks against civilian objects, that is, objects which are not military objectives', again in the context of an international armed conflict. The elements of this crime are:

1. The perpetrator directed an attack.
2. The object of the attack was civilian objects: that is, objects which are not military objectives.
3. The perpetrator intended such civilian objects to be the object of the attack.
4. The conduct took place in the context of and was associated with an international armed conflict.
5. The perpetrator was aware of factual circumstances that established the existence of an armed conflict.[26]

Under both these crimes, the perpetrator will be whomever the Court determines 'directed the attack', which could involve anyone in the chain of command, including the person who authorized the attack and the person who actually carried out the physical act of launching the attack (that is, through a particular weapons system). In the context of a nuclear weapon, the person who directed the attack could include anyone vested with the power to authorize a nuclear attack (that is, a head of government or high-level governmental panel), as well as any military unit or personnel who launched the attack (that is, whoever was responsible for entering targeting data and for *physically* launching the weapon – for instance, from a submarine, aircraft or land-based silo). Moreover, issues regarding command responsibility arise, such that a commander of the unit that launched a nuclear attack against civilians or civilian objects could be responsible for ordering an illegal attack, as well as failing to prevent or repress the commission of an illegal attack – something discussed in more detail later in this section.

For the crime of attacking civilians, the perpetrator will be guilty if they intended to make the civilian population (or individual civilians not taking direct part in hostilities) the object of attack, *knowing* that the attack was being directed against a civilian rather than a military target. The crime of attacking civilian objects is made out if the perpetrator has directed the attack against an object knowing it is a civilian object and not a military objective. In the

25 Elements of Crimes, art 8(2)(b)(i).

26 Elements of Crimes, art 8(2)(b)(ii).

context of nuclear weapons, intentionally launching an attack against a civilian object with a nuclear weapon would be a war crime.

The Rome Statute criminalizes attacking civilians and persons *hors de combat* in non-international armed conflicts in Article 8(2)(e)(i), with the elements of crime in a non-international armed conflict essentially identical to those in an international armed conflict (merely replacing 'in the context of . . . an international armed conflict' with 'in the context of . . . an armed conflict not of an international character'). There is no war crime of intentionally targeting civilian objects in a non-international armed conflict, but there is the war crime of intentionally 'directing attacks against buildings dedicated to religion, education, art, science or charitable purposes, historic monuments, hospitals and places where the sick and wounded are collected, provided they are not military objectives' in a non-international armed conflict in Article 8(2)(e)(iv).

For the crime of intentionally attacking protected objects (that is, buildings dedicated to religion, education, art, and so on) in a non-international armed conflict, the elements are functionally identical to those of the crime of intentionally attacking civilian objects in an international armed conflict, with the only difference being that the protected objects are listed (that is, buildings dedicated to religion, education, art, and so on), and the attack must take place in the context of a non-international armed conflict.

As Boothby and Heintschel von Heinegg have noted, the prospect of nuclear weapons being used in a non-international armed conflict is unlikely but not impossible;[27] an armed non-State group may be able to acquire a nuclear weapon, or a State may choose to use a nuclear weapon against an armed non-State group operating in territory not its own. Were a non-State armed group able to acquire a weapon (or if such a weapon were used in the context of a non-international armed conflict), Article 8(2)(e)(iv) could potentially be triggered.

6.3.2 Causing Excessive Incidental Death, Injury, or Damage

Article 8(2)(b)(iv) establishes that it is a war crime, in an international armed conflict, to intentionally launch

> an attack in the knowledge that such attack will cause incidental loss of life or injury to civilians or damage to civilian objects or widespread, long-term and severe damage to the natural environment which would be clearly excessive in relation to the concrete and direct overall military advantage anticipated.[28]

27 Boothby and Heintschel von Heinegg, *Nuclear Weapons Law*, 73.
28 Rome Statute, art 8(2)(b)(iv).

The elements of this crime are:

1. The perpetrator launched an attack.
2. The attack was such that it would cause incidental death or injury to civilians or damage to civilian objects or widespread, long-term, and severe damage to the natural environment and that such death, injury or damage would be of such an extent as to be clearly excessive in relation to the concrete and direct overall military advantage anticipated.
3. The perpetrator knew the attack would cause incidental death or injury to civilians or damage to civilian objects or widespread, long-term, and severe damage to the natural environment and that such death, injury, or damage would be of such an extent as to be clearly excessive in relation to the concrete and direct overall military advantage anticipated.
4. The conduct took place in the context of and was associated with an international armed conflict.
5. The perpetrator was aware of factual circumstances that established the existence of an armed conflict.[29]

Article 8(2)(b)(iv) thus criminalizes attacks that are a breach of the principle and rule of proportionality, as codified in Article 51(5)(b) (and referenced in Article 57) of API. It is noteworthy that an attack that causes excessive damage to the natural environment is captured by the rule (unless part of the natural environment could be considered a military objective). Additionally, the damage caused by the attack must be 'clearly' excessive, which suggests that the incidental injury and damage must be notably greater that the anticipated military advantage such that 'no reasonable decision-maker would have decided to proceed with the attack'.[30] Finally, the perpetrator must *know* that the attack will cause excessive incidental injury and damage.

The 'persons who launch the attack' presumably include the person who physically launched the weapon (e.g. the pilot, captain, or commander of the nuclear-armed craft). Additionally, any launching personnel would have to know that the attack would cause incidental death or injury to civilians or damage to civilian objects or widespread, long-term, and severe damage to the natural environment that is clearly excessive when compared with the concrete and direct overall military advantage anticipated. Making this determination would depend entirely on what kinds of information the launching personnel were privy to and at what stage.

29 Elements of Crimes, art 8(2)(b)(iv).
30 Boothby and Heintschel von Heinegg, *Nuclear Weapons Law*, 276.

6.3.3 Employing Poison or Poison Weapons

Finally, as argued by Boothby and Heintschel von Heinegg,[31] it is open to the ICC to characterize nuclear weapons as employing poison or being poison weapons, the use of which is a war crime in both international[32] and non-international[33] armed conflict. The elements of the crime are that:

1. The perpetrator employed a substance or a weapon that releases a substance as a result of its employment.
2. The substance was such that it causes death or serious damage to health in the ordinary course of events, through its toxic properties.
3. The conduct took place in the context of and was associated with an international armed conflict.
4. The perpetrator was aware of factual circumstances that established the existence of an armed conflict.[34]

On detonation, nuclear weapons release radiation and radioactive debris that can potentially cause illness or death to persons exposed to such radioactivity. As Boothby and Heintschel von Heinegg observe, '[i]t would be arguable that it is the toxic properties of the radioactive debris and radiation that, "in the ordinary course of events", cause death or serious damage to health'.[35] While the ICC may yet characterize nuclear weapons as poison weapons, State practice in relation to the possession of nuclear weapons would not seem to support such a conclusion.[36]

In the context of a nuclear attack, and for the purposes of an NC3 code of conduct, a nuclear attack could amount to the previously listed war crimes, so long as the constituent elements were made out. Therefore, any State NC3 should ensure that any personnel engaged in nuclear operations are instructed in the law regarding war crimes and when participation in nuclear operations might amount to such a crime.

6.4 A Note on Command Responsibility

Finally, the question of command responsibility arises in relation to international criminal law. The law is complex, but essentially, a commander may

31 Boothby and Heintschel von Heinegg, *Nuclear Weapons Law*, 277–278.

32 Rome Statute, art 8(2)(b)(xvii).

33 Rome Statute, art 8(2)(e)(xiii).

34 Elements of Crimes, art 8(2)(b)(xvii).

35 Boothby and Heintschel von Heinegg, *Nuclear Weapons Law*, 278.

36 On State practice with regard to poison weapons, see further the ICRC, Customary IHL Database, Rule 72: Poison, https://ihl-databases.icrc.org/en/customary-ihl/v1/rule72. With regard to nuclear weapons, see further ICRC, Customary IHL Database, Nuclear Weapons, https://ihl-databases.icrc.org/en/customary-ihl/v1/nuwe.

find themselves culpable under international criminal law if they either order subordinates to carry out an act criminalized under international criminal law or fail to prevent or repress the commission of an illegal attack by subordinates. As outlined in Article 28 of the Rome Statute:

(a) A military commander or person effectively acting as a military commander shall be criminally responsible for crimes within the jurisdiction of the Court committed by forces under his or her effective command and control, or effective authority and control as the case may be, as a result of his or her failure to exercise control properly over such forces, where:

  (i) That military commander or person either knew or, owing to the circumstances at the time, should have known that the forces were committing or about to commit such crimes; and
  (ii) That military commander or person failed to take all necessary and reasonable measures within his or her power to prevent or repress their commission or to submit the matter to the competent authorities for investigation and prosecution.

(b) With respect to superior and subordinate relationships not described in paragraph (a), a superior shall be criminally responsible for crimes within the jurisdiction of the Court committed by subordinates under his or her effective authority and control, as a result of his or her failure to exercise control properly over such subordinates, where:

  (i) The superior either knew, or consciously disregarded information which clearly indicated, that the subordinates were committing or about to commit such crimes;
  (ii) The crimes concerned activities that were within the effective responsibility and control of the superior; and
  (iii) The superior failed to take all necessary and reasonable measures within his or her power to prevent or repress their commission or to submit the matter to the competent authorities for investigation and prosecution.

Under international criminal law, the orders to carry out an illegal act cannot be used as a defence. As noted in Article 33 of the Rome Statute:

1. The fact that a crime within the jurisdiction of the Court has been committed by a person pursuant to an order of a Government or of a superior, whether military or civilian, shall not relieve that person of criminal responsibility unless:

  (a) The person was under a legal obligation to obey orders of the Government or the superior in question;
  (b) The person did not know that the order was unlawful; and
  (c) The order was not manifestly unlawful.

2. For the purposes of this article, orders to commit genocide or crimes against humanity are manifestly unlawful.

For command responsibility to be found, all three elements must exist cumulatively: 1) the legal obligation to follow orders, 2) the lack of awareness that the order is illegal, and 3) the absence of a manifestly unlawful order. Any State NC3 would need to ensure that nuclear weapons personnel are thus appropriately instructed in the law on command responsibility and that orders to commit genocide or crimes against humanity are always considered manifestly unlawful such that criminal responsibility for such acts is not excused.

Previous chapters have outlined relevant laws applicable to nuclear operations in which any NC3 architecture must exist. However, there is no extant international law that dictates how a State should *structure* its NC3. Given that any nuclear (and, indeed, non-nuclear) State requires a robust NC3 at its centre, it might be considered a vital necessity for a binding international agreement governing NC3.

Unfortunately, States (in particular nuclear States) are increasingly reluctant to commit to multilateral treaties on complex issues, especially those relating to security and sovereignty. Arguably, the possibility of reaching consensus on the safest and most secure NC3 architecture is illusory. However, States may be willing to commit to non-binding instruments, which nonetheless have proven influential in shaping State behaviour and in achieving broad consensus that eventually evolves into binding customary law. Drawing on the wealth of practice and theory on the topic of non-binding norms and informal international lawmaking, the following chapter will investigate what is needed to create such an instrument and to ensure its success.

7 Lessons From Non-Binding Instruments

This review of international law reveals a substantial body of international rules governing the use of nuclear weapons, including on permissible targets, precautions in attack, and obligations to take constant care while targeting. There are also extensive rules governing when a State may legally have the right to use force (potentially including nuclear weapons) and rules defining and criminally sanctioning war crimes, crimes against humanity, and acts of genocide. Alongside these rules are other regional security regimes. This law sits alongside differing State practice regarding the structure of each nuclear weapons State's NC3, which is itself informed by each State's strategic and policy objectives.

From the survey and analysis of international law and State practice regarding nuclear weapons and nuclear weapons systems, it is also clear that there is no specific *lex lata* at international law – either treaty or custom – that dictates *how* a State should configure its NC3. While some States follow acceptably 'good' practices regarding NC3, there is no existing international law that *obligates* nuclear weapons States to follow such practices.

Given the culture of confidentiality that exists surrounding State NC3, it is unlikely that States would agree to international treaty requirements on how to configure their NC3 systems. Any hope for consistent systematization of NC3 among nuclear States must come through other informal sources of international lawmaking, such as non-binding instruments.[1] As this chapter will explore, States may be more willing to adopt a set of rules that have instructive if not binding force regarding NC3.

7.1 The Turn to Informal International Lawmaking

That an NC3 instrument should be adopted in non-binding form at first appears counter-intuitive – surely, given the centrality of a robust NC3 to a

1 See Joost Pauwelyn, Ramses Wessel, and Jan Wouters (eds), *Informal International Lawmaking* (Oxford University Press, 2012).

DOI: 10.4324/9781003759294-7

State's nuclear security, States would want to adopt binding rules to ensure their sovereign rights and national security needs are protected, and they can be assured that other nuclear States are likewise establishing safe and robust NC3. However, there are two compelling reasons why States would not want to adopt a treaty dictating how to establish their NC3.

First, the culture of secrecy surrounding the NC3 of many States suggests that States would not wish to have this information publicly known in its entirety. Second, given that an NC3 is intricately tied up with State sovereignty, again, States would be unwilling to accept binding rules that might impinge on their sovereign prerogative regarding national security and defence decision-making.

However, a *non-binding* NC3 instrument would be in keeping with current international lawmaking trends, particularly in relation to laws of armed conflict. In recent years, there has been a move away from binding multilateral treaties toward instruments of less-than-treaty status.[2] As noted by Janssens and Wouters, 'Over the last two decades, international humanitarian law (IHL) has witnessed an increasing reluctance on the part of States to adopt or amend treaties, recognize customary international rules or even become formally involved in the further development of IHL'.[3] As highlighted by Hughes and Shereshevsky, 'formal international lawmaking has reached a nadir'[4] due to 'global stagnation and great power competition increasingly preclud[ing] access to the formal methods of international lawmaking'.[5] In the complex security and political environment of the 21st century, States seem to be turning increasingly to instruments of less-than-treaty status to provide guiderails for international relations.

If States are therefore reluctant to adopt or develop binding norms in relation to armed conflict and other security situations, other methods of rulemaking might logically address existing gaps. However, some obvious questions arise: How valuable are rules if they are non-binding? Do non-binding instruments have any actual impact on how States behave? Does the absence of sanctions for breaches render such instruments moot?

2 For further analysis, see Curtis A Bradley, Jack L Goldsmith, and Oona A Hathaway, 'The Rise of Nonbinding International Agreements: An Empirical, Comparative, and Normative Analysis' (2023) 90 *University of Chicago Law Review* 1281; Peter Vedel Kessing, 'The Use of Soft Law in Regulating Armed Conflict: From *Jus in Bello* to "Soft Law *in Bello*"?', in Stéphanie Lagoutte, Thomas Gammeltoft-Hansen, and John Cerrone (eds), *Tracing the Roles of Soft Law in Human Rights* (Oxford University Press, 2016); Andreas Motzfeldt Kravik, 'An Analysis of Stagnation in Multilateral Law-Making – and Why the Law of the Sea Has Transcended the Stagnation Trend' (2021) 34 *Leiden Journal of International Law* 935; David Hughes and Yahli Shereshevsky, 'State-Academic Lawmaking' (2023) 64 *Harvard International Law Journal* 253.

3 Pauline Charlotte Janssens and Jan Wouters, 'Informal International Law-Making: A Way Around the Deadlock of International Humanitarian Law?' (2022) 104 *International Review of the Red Cross* 2111, 2112.

4 Hughes and Shereshevsky, 'State-Academic Lawmaking', 257.

5 Hughes and Shereshevsky, 'State-Academic Lawmaking', 253.

To answer these questions, this chapter will examine informal international lawmaking and the production of non-binding norms at international law. It will explore definitional questions regarding non-binding norms, the methods and reasons for their creation, how they have been received in practice, and their effectiveness in shaping State behaviour without binding force. The chapter will also investigate whether it is possible to discern any consistent underlying characteristics in well-received and influential non-binding instruments to consider why such instruments have been successful in changing or influencing State behaviour, despite their non-binding character.

Drawing on the author's own extensive research in the area,[6] the chapter will look at several non-binding instruments that have been adopted to guide the practice of States in the conduct of armed conflicts and other international security activities. These findings will set the groundwork for the final part of this study – a proposed code of conduct for State NC3.

7.1.1 What Is Informal International Lawmaking?

Before exploring the normative power of non-binding instruments in international law, it is worth briefly investigating definitional issues surrounding non-binding norms and informal international lawmaking and the history of non-binding instruments as a central part of current and past international law. For example, quintessential non-binding instruments include resolutions of the UN General Assembly,[7] draft articles or reports of the International Law Commission,[8] and recommendations of UN organs.[9] Non-binding instruments have played pivotal roles in the progressive development of varied

6 Emily Crawford, *Non-Binding Norms in International Humanitarian Law: Efficacy, Legitimacy, and Legality* (Oxford University Press, 2021).

7 Charter of the United Nations, opened for signature 26 June 1945, entered into force 24 October 1945, XV UNCIO 355, art 10: 'The General Assembly may discuss any questions or any matters within the scope of the present Charter or relating to the powers and functions of any organs provided for in the present Charter, and, except as provided in Article 12, may make recommendations to the Members of the United Nations or to the Security Council or to both on any such questions or matters'. See, for example, UN General Assembly, *Resolution 2444 (XXIII): Respect for Human Rights in Armed Conflicts*, UN Doc A/RES/2444(XXIII) (19 December 1968).

8 For example, Articles on the Responsibility of States for Internationally Wrongful Acts (ARSIWA), in International Law Commission, *Report of the International Law Commission on the Work of Its Fifty-third Session (23 April–1 June and 2 July–10 August 2001)*, UN Doc A/56/10 (2001).

9 See General Comments made by UN human rights bodies, such as the UN Human Rights Committee, *General Comment No 36 on Article 6: Right to Life*, UN Doc CCPR/C/GC/36 (3 September 2019).

international law fields, including international environmental law,[10] international economic law,[11] and international human rights law.[12]

Generally considered to fall under 'soft law',[13] non-binding instruments are defined by scholars and practitioners as 'those international norms, principles, and procedures' which fall outside formal sources (e.g. Article 38, paragraph 1 of the ICJ Statute) that lack 'the requisite normative content to create enforceable rights and obligations'[14] and do not engage the 'legal responsibility'[15] of their addressees. Nevertheless, such instruments 'have the characteristics of "law" [and a directive effect on the will] . . . of those to whom the "soft law" is addressed',[16] and, while such instruments have no legally binding force, they 'nevertheless may have practical effects'.[17]

The process of making soft law instruments must be considered as part of a larger movement known as 'informal international lawmaking'– a term coined in 2012 by Joost Pauwelyn, Ramses Wessel, and Jan Wouters[18] to describe the process of:

> Cross-border cooperation between public authorities, with or without the participation of private actors and/or international organizations, in a forum other than a traditional international organization (process informality), and/or as between actors other than traditional diplomatic actors (such as regulators or agencies) (actor informality) and/or which does not result

10 For example, the Rio Declaration on Environment and Development, 14 June 1992, 31 ILM 874, in United Nations, *Report of the United Nations Conference on Environment and Development*, vol I, UN Doc A/CONF.151/26 (1993).

11 For example, the Helsinki Final Act, Conference on Security and Co-Operation in Europe (1 August 1975), www.osce.org/files/f/documents/5/c/39501.pdf.

12 Such as UN General Assembly, *Resolution 217A (III): Universal Declaration of Human Rights*, UN Doc A/RES/217(III) (10 December 1948).

13 For an assessment of the differing approaches to and definitions of soft law, see RR Baxter, 'International Law in "Her Infinite Variety"' (1980) 29 *International & Comparative Law Quarterly* 549; Jaye Ellis, 'Shades of Grey: Soft Law and the Validity of Public International Law' (2012) 25 *Leiden Journal of International Law* 313, 315–323; Andrew T Guzman and Timothy Meyer, 'Soft Law', in Eugene Kontorovich and Francesco Parisi (eds), *Economic Analysis of International Law* (Edward Elgar, 2015), 123–127.

14 Francesco Francioni, 'International "Soft Law": A Contemporary Assessment', in Vaughan Lowe and Malgosia Fitzmaurice (eds), *Fifty Years of the International Court of Justice: Essays in Honour of Sir Robert Jennings* (Cambridge University Press, 1996), 168.

15 Oscar Schachter, 'The Twilight Existence of Nonbinding International Agreements' (1977) 71 *American Journal of International Law* 296, 300.

16 AJP Tammes, 'Soft Law', in TMC Asser Institute (ed), *Essays on International & Comparative Law in Honour of Judge Erades* (Martinus Nijhoff Publishers, 1983), 187.

17 Francis Snyder, 'Soft Law and Institutional Practice in the European Community', in Stephen Martin (ed), *The Construction of Europe: Essays in Honour of Emile Noël* (Kluwer, 1994), 198. See also Francis Snyder, 'The Effectiveness of European Community Law: Institutions, Processes, Tools and Techniques' (1993) 56 *Modern Law Review* 19, 32.

18 Pauwelyn, Wessel, and Wouters, *Informal International Lawmaking*.

in a formal treaty or other traditional source of international law (output informality).[19]

Informal international lawmaking is any process of generating rules that involve 'new actors, processes and instruments that escape the confines of traditional international law'.[20] Informal international lawmaking can therefore involve several kinds and combinations of international actor, from the State to civil society to non-governmental or intergovernmental organizations to academics – indeed, any non-State actor. Likewise, the processes employed to generate informal international law need not resemble conventional diplomatic conferences where treaties are drafted, nor do the ultimate outcomes of such processes need to resemble treaties in substance.

Despite their non-binding nature, soft law documents have been largely well received and influential in practice. Specific instruments of less-than-treaty status have influenced State behaviour, either through practical means (that is, the State has changed its behaviour to align with the soft law instrument and has stated the instrument as an instigating cause), because the instrument has become part of the lingua franca of State practice (that is, the instrument is referred to and included in the State's corpus of rules of conduct – for instance, by inclusion in military manuals), or because instruments of the State have called upon these documents as sources of obligation (that is, in court cases). Some of the instruments will be explored in more detail in the next section, to better trace and map commonalities that have contributed to their success in practice.

7.2 Non-Binding Instruments in the Law of Armed Conflict

For comparison purposes, three different types of non-binding instruments are examined to demonstrate all aspects of informal international lawmaking processes: the *San Remo Manual on International Law Applicable to Armed Conflicts at Sea* (1995);[21] the ICRC study on *Customary International Humanitarian Law* (2005) (ICRC CIHL Study);[22] and the Montreux Document on Pertinent International Legal Obligations and Good Practices for States Related to Operations of Private Military and Security Companies

19 Joost Pauwelyn, 'Informal International Lawmaking: Framing the Concept and Research Questions', in Joost Pauwelyn, Wessel, and Wouters (eds), *Informal International Lawmaking* (Oxford University Press, 2012), 22.

20 Eva Kassoti, 'Beyond State Consent? International Legal Scholarship and the Challenge of Informal International Law-Making' (2016) 63 *Netherlands International Law Review* 99, 99–100.

21 Louise Doswald-Beck (ed), *San Remo Manual on International Law Applicable to Armed Conflicts at Sea* (Cambridge University Press, 1995).

22 Jean-Marie Henckaerts and Louise Doswald-Beck (eds), *Customary International Humanitarian Law* (Cambridge University Press, 2005).

During Armed Conflict (2008)[23] and its connected instrument, the International Code of Conduct for Private Security Service Providers (2010).[24]

These instruments were chosen because all demonstrate different aspects of informal international lawmaking processes, through either informal process,[25] informal output,[26] or 'actor informality'[27] – the involvement of stakeholders and participants other than States. For example, the *San Remo Manual* is an instrument whose creation was largely driven by civil society, including academics and practitioners.[28] However, the *Manual* also had a form of State engagement – some participants in the San Remo process were serving military personnel (who, however, attended only in their personal capacity). The *San Remo Manual* was intended to be *lex lata* and not, for the most part, an exercise in progressive development of the law.

The ICRC CIHL study was a purely civil society–driven document, albeit by a civil society organization with a unique international legal personality, and is specially tasked with the affirmation and development of international humanitarian law.[29] The result of extensive consultation with experts and comprehensive analysis of State practice, the final publication was a detailed report on the customary rules of international humanitarian law applicable in both international and non-international armed conflict, analysing the practice of States[30] and relevant practice connected to international and intergovern-

23 Montreux Document on Pertinent International Legal Obligations and Good Practices for States Related to Operations of Private Military and Security Companies During Armed Conflict, 17 September 2008.

24 International Code of Conduct for Private Security Service Providers, 10 November 2010,

25 Ayelet Berman and Ramses A Wessel, 'The International Legal Form and Status of Informal International Lawmaking Bodies: Consequences for Accountability', in Pauwelyn, Wessel, and Wouters (eds), *Informal International Lawmaking*, 36.

26 Berman and Wessel, 'The International Legal Form and Status of Informal International Lawmaking Bodies'.

27 Berman and Wessel, 'The International Legal Form and Status of Informal International Lawmaking Bodies'.

28 ICRC, *Resolution VII: Work on International Humanitarian Law in Armed Conflicts at Sea and on Land*, adopted at the final plenary meeting on 31 October 1986, 25th International Conference of the Red Cross, Geneva, 23–31 October 1986, reprinted in (1986) 26 *International Review of the Red Cross* 340, 349. For discussion of the involvement in the *San Remo Manual of the Institute of International Humanitarian* Law, the ICRC, and the Universities of Pisa and Syracuse, see Louise Doswald-Beck, 'The San Remo Manual on International Law Applicable to Armed Conflicts at Sea' (1995) 89 *American Journal of International Law* 192.

29 ICRC, *Resolution 1: International Humanitarian Law: From Law to Action, Report on the Follow-up to the International Conference for the Protection of War Victims*, 26th International Conference of the Red Cross and Red Crescent, Geneva, 3–7 December 1995, reprinted in (1996) 310 *International Review of the Red Cross* 58.

30 The Study included in its ambit the State practice found in 'military manuals, national legislation, national case-law, instructions to armed and security forces, military communiqués during war, diplomatic protests, opinions of official legal advisers, comments by governments on draft treaties, executive decisions and regulations, pleadings before international tribunals, statements in international organisations and at international conferences and government positions taken with respect to resolutions of international organisations': ICRC, Customary IHL Database, Introduction, https://ihl-databases.icrc.org/en/customary-ihl/v1/in.

mental organizations.[31] The final document was intended as a statement of the customary *lex lata* regarding international humanitarian law rules – in particular, those adopted following the Geneva Conventions of 1949.

The Montreux Document was the result of a process[32] started in late 2005 by the ICRC, working in conjunction with the Swiss Federal Department of Foreign Affairs.[33] Primarily involving State representatives (with some limited engagement with representatives from the private military and security industry[34] and independent subject matter experts),[35] the Montreux Document drew on existing international,[36] regional,[37] and domestic[38] laws and codes of conduct, including the Geneva Conventions and the ICRC CIHL Study. Even though non-State actors were involved in the early stages, the Montreux instrument was eventually adopted as an intergovernmental statement only. Part I of the document (on relevant international law, international humanitarian law,

31 Including the United Nations, the Organisation of African Unity/African Union, the Council of Europe, the Gulf Cooperation Council, the European Union, the League of Arab States, the Organization of American States, the Organisation of the Islamic Conference, and the Organization for Security and Co-operation in Europe, as well as the practice of the Commonwealth of Independent States, the Inter-Parliamentary Union, and the Non-Aligned Movement. Additionally, the practice of the UN Security Council, General Assembly, and Commission on Human Rights was examined, as were ad hoc UN investigations, work undertaken by the International Law Commission (as well as comments in response to Commission work), UN General Assembly committee work, reports from the UN Secretary-General, reporting procedures under various international treaty regimes (such as the Committee against Torture), the *travaux préparatoires* of treaties, State submissions before international and regional courts, and international case law (to the extent that such case law provided evidence of the existence of custom).

32 Known as the 'Swiss Initiative'. See Marie-Louise Tougas, 'Some Comments and Observations on the Montreux Document' (2009) 12 *Yearbook of International Humanitarian Law* 312; James Cockayne, 'Regulating Private Military and Security Companies: The Content, Negotiation, Weaknesses and Promise of the Montreux Document' (2008) 13 *Journal of Conflict and Security Law* 401.

33 For a detailed history of the process, see Montreux Document Forum, 'Historical Timeline'.

34 From the companies themselves, as well as from industry associations in the United States and the United Kingdom.

35 Swiss Federal Department of Foreign Affairs, Directorate of International Law, *Expert Meeting of Governmental and Other Experts on Private Military and Security Companies*, 13–14 November 2006, Montreux, Chair's Summary (22 July 2007); Swiss Federal Department of Foreign Affairs, Directorate of International Law, *Workshop of Governmental Experts and Industry Representatives on Private Military/Security Companies*, 16–17 January 2006, Zurich, Summary of the Chair (1 September 2006).

36 Including the International Peace Operations Association Code of Conduct; the UN Basic Principles on the Use of Force and Firearms by Law Enforcement Officials, 7 September 1990; and the UN Code of Conduct for Law Enforcement Officials, 17 December 1979. See Swiss Federal Department of Foreign Affairs, Directorate of International Law, *Workshop of Governmental Experts and Industry Representatives on Private Military/Security Companies*, 16–17 January 2006, Zurich, Summary of the Chair (1 September 2006).

37 Including the EU Code of Conduct on Arms Exports, Doc 8675/2/98 Rev 2 (5 June 1988); the Commonwealth of Independent States Model Law on Countering Mercenarism (19 November 2005); the CoESS and UNI-Europa Code of Conduct and Ethics for the Private Security Sector (July 2003); and the Sarajevo Code of Conduct and Client Procurement Guidelines (August 2006).

38 Including from Afghanistan, Angola, Australia, Canada, France, Iraq, Sierra Leone, South Africa, the United Kingdom, and the United States. See Cockayne, 'Regulating Private Military and Security Companies'.

and international human rights law obligations regarding private military and security companies [PMSCs]) was intended to be a statement of *lex lata*, with Part II a statement of 'best practice'. The 'partner' instrument to Montreux, the International Code of Conduct for Private Security Service Providers, was adopted in 2010 following an initiative by the Swiss government[39] to adapt and adopt the Montreux rules to create a set of guidelines for private military and security companies themselves. Drafting involved the participation of the private security industry, civil society and academia, and States and international organizations. The final document is a mix of both *lex lata* and *lex ferenda*.

These instruments have been chosen as case studies for an additional reason: they demonstrate quite clearly how a non-binding instrument can influence, and even outright change, State behaviour. As the following sections demonstrate, these instruments have, in some instances, asserted the existence of a rule as *lex lata*, even when the legal status of such a rule has been in doubt (that is, because the purported rule might be closer to *lex ferenda*, or a hortatory injunction at best), only for States to then acknowledge and accept the rule as having *lex lata* standing. The process of codifying the rule (and, importantly, who codified it, why, and in what context) seems to have gone some way to transforming a recommendation into something more compulsory, which suggests that non-binding instruments, if they hew to certain processes regarding their formation, can have as much impact as binding instruments.

39 In conjunction with the Geneva Academy of International Humanitarian Law and Human Rights, an educational institution established in 2007, and the Geneva Centre for the Democratic Control of Armed Forces (DCAF), a civil society institution which 'assists partner states in developing laws, institutions, policies and practices to improve the governance of their security sector through inclusive and participatory reforms based on international norms and good practices . . . [and] advises governments and international organizations in designing and implementing their own programmes for supporting states in developing their security sector governance. DCAF creates innovative knowledge products, promotes norms and good practices, and provides legal and policy advice. DCAF supports capacity building of state, civil society, and private sector stakeholders by providing access to independent expertise and information on Security Sector Governance and Reform (SSG/R)': DCAF, 'What Is DCAF?', www.dcaf.ch/about-us.

7.2.1 The San Remo Manual on Naval Warfare

Widely cited in domestic[40] and international[41] courts as an 'authoritative commentary'[42] on naval warfare law, the *San Remo Manual* is routinely employed in domestic[43] and international[44] commissions of inquiry, tribunals,[45] and other

40 *Horgan v an Taoiseach* [2003] 2 IR 468.

41 *Oil Platforms (Islamic Republic of Iran v United States of America)*, ICJ, Rejoinder submitted by the United States of America (23 March 2001), 6.44–6.49; Counter-Memorial and Counter-Claim submitted by the United States of America (23 June 1997), 136; Reply and Defence to Counter-Claim submitted by the Islamic Republic of Iran (10 March 1999), vol I, 151–153, 204–205; Further Response to the United States' Counter-Claim submitted by the Islamic Republic of Iran (24 September 2001), vol I, 92, 95, 98, 102; Public sitting held on Wednesday 26 February 2003, at 3 pm, at the Peace Palace, President Shi presiding, ICJ, Verbatim Record 2003/13, 39; *Situation on the Registered Vessels of the Union of the Comoros, the Hellenic Republic and the Kingdom of Cambodia*, Pre-Trial Chamber I, ICC-01/13 (23 June 2015), 41, 42, 45; *Situation on the Registered Vessels of the Union of the Comoros, the Hellenic Republic and the Kingdom of Cambodia*, Pre-Trial Chamber, Corrigendum of Annex, Partly Dissenting Opinion of Judge Péter Kovács, ICC-01/13-34-Anx-Corr (16 July 2015), 15–16; *Situation on the Registered Vessels of the Union of the Comoros, the Hellenic Republic and the Kingdom of Cambodia*, Pre-Trial Chamber I, Public Redacted Version of Prosecution's Consolidated Response to the Observations of the Victims, ICC-01/13-29-Red (14 July 2015), 47; Referral of the 'Union of the Comoros' with respect to the 31 May 2010 Israeli raid on the Humanitarian Aid Flotilla bound for Gaza Strip, requesting the Prosecutor of the International Criminal Court pursuant to Articles 12, 13 and 14 of the Rome Statute to initiate an investigation into the crimes committed within the Court's jurisdiction, arising from this raid (14 May 2013); ICC, *Situation on Registered Vessels of Comoros, Greece and Cambodia: Article 53(1) Report* (6 November 2014); *Situation on the Registered Vessels of the Union of the Comoros, the Hellenic Republic and the Kingdom of Cambodia*, Pre-Trial Chamber I, Appendix B: Letter Dated 30 September 2014 from Der Generalbundesanwalt Beim Bundesgerichtschof to Frau Inge Höger, MdB Followed by Unofficial Translation of Letter into English, ICC-01/13-45-AnxB (13 August 2015).

42 *Alseran v Ministry of Defence* [2019] QB 1251, para 96.

43 Turkish National Commission of Inquiry, *Report on the Israeli Attack on the Humanitarian Aid Convoy to Gaza on 31 May 2010* (February 2011), 7, 60–64, 68–69, 83–84, 87–88, 93, 95, 98, 100, 103; Public Commission to Examine the Maritime Incident of 31 May 2010 (Turkel Commission), *Report, Part 1* (January 2011), 42–45, 49, 59–60, 82–86, 90–91, 93–94, 103, 109, 110, 115.

44 UN Office for the Coordination of Humanitarian Affairs, *Oxford Guidance on the Law Relating to Humanitarian Relief Operations in Situations of Armed Conflict* (OCHA, 2016), 36–37; International Law Commission, *Report of the International Law Commission on the Work of Its Sixty-third Session (26 April–3 June and 4 July–12 August 2011)*, UN Doc A/66/10 (2011), 354; International Law Commission, *Second Report on the Protection of the Environment in Relation to Armed Conflicts, Submitted by Marie G Jacobsson, Special Rapporteur*, Sixty-seventh Session, 4 May–5 June and 6 July–7 August 2015, UN Doc A/CN.4/685 (28 May 2015), 55–56; Geoffrey Palmer, Alvaro Uribe, Joseph Ciechanover Itzhar, and Süleyman Özdem Sanberk, *Report of the Secretary-General's Panel of Inquiry on the 31 May 2010 Flotilla Incident* (July 2011), 5.

45 Eritrea-Ethiopia Claims Commission, Final Award, *Ports – Ethiopia's Claim 6* (19 December 2005), para 24; Eritrea-Ethiopia Claims Commission, Partial Award, *Western Front, Aerial Bombardment and Related Claims – Eritrea's Claims 1, 3, 5, 9–13, 14, 21, 25 & 26* (19 December 2005), Eritrea's Claim 25, Separate Opinion, para 3.

intergovernmental forums.[46]Additionally, the *Manual* has been cited in the military manuals of several States[47] and was commended by the ICR[48] as 'a valid restatement of customary and treaty international law applicable to armed conflicts at sea'.[49]

Considering there had been no treaty on naval warfare in the law of armed conflict for decades,[50] the *San Remo Manual* constituted an overdue extension of and development for naval warfare laws. Reference to the conduct of naval warfare (as opposed to protections for naval military personnel) was similarly limited in other international humanitarian law instruments.

The *San Remo Manual* innovated the concept of so-called 'exclusion zones': 'rules applicable to zones which belligerents might establish and which adversely affect the use by others of certain areas of the sea'.[51] The inclusion of these paragraphs generated 'a certain amount of controversy amongst the participants as to whether rules applicable to such zones should be included in the Manual, for it was feared that doing so could encourage the belief that they are clearly lawful'.[52]

State practice in relation to exclusion zones prior to the adoption of the *San Remo Manual* was mixed, with some evidence of States engaging in establishing exclusion zones and other States treating exclusion zones as clearly unlawful under international law.[53]

46 UN Human Rights Council, *Report of the International Fact-Finding Mission to Investigate Violations of International Law, Including International Humanitarian and Human Rights Law, Resulting from the Israeli Attacks on the Flotilla of Ships Carrying Humanitarian Assistance*, UN Doc A/HRC/15/21 (27 September 2010), 9, 12–14; Palmer et al, *Report of the Secretary-General's Panel of Inquiry*, 5, 15, 18, 22–23, 29–29, 34, 70–71, 73, 79–80, 81, 84–96, https://unispal.un.org/pdfs/GazaFlotillaPanelReport.pdf.

47 See AR Thomas and James C Duncan (eds), *Annotated Supplement to the Commander's Handbook on the Law of Naval Operations*, reprinted in *International Law Studies*, vol 73 (Naval War College, 1999), 301, 392, 412, 416; UK Ministry of Defence, *The Joint Service Manual of the Law of Armed Conflict* (JSP 383, 2004), ch 13; Norway, *Manual i krigens folkerett* [Manual on the International Law of War] (2013), 99, 168, 198. See also Danish Ministry of Defence, *Military Manual on International Law Relevant to Danish Armed Forces in International Operations* (updated 12 October 2020), which includes more than 100 footnotes referencing the *San Remo Manual*).

48 ICRC, *Commentary on the Second Geneva Convention: Convention (II) for the Amelioration of the Condition of the Wounded, Sick and Shipwrecked Members of Armed Forces at Sea* (2nd ed, 2017), https://ihl-databases.icrc.org/en/ihl-treaties/gcii-1949?activeTab=1949GCs-APs-and-commentaries.

49 ICRC, *Commentary on the Second Geneva Convention: Convention (II) for the Amelioration of the Condition of the Wounded, Sick and Shipwrecked Members of Armed Forces at Sea*, para 115.

50 See ICRC, 'Air and Naval Warfare', www.icrc.org/en/law-and-policy/air-and-naval-warfare.

51 'Explanation', in Doswald-Beck, *San Remo Manual*, 69.

52 Explanation', in Doswald-Beck *San Remo Manual*, 69.

53 On the practice regarding exclusion zones prior to and following the adoption of the *San Remo Manual*, see generally Wolff Heintschel von Heinegg, 'The Law of Armed Conflict at Sea', in Dieter Fleck (ed), *The Handbook of International Humanitarian Law* (3rd ed, Oxford University Press, 2013), 522–524.

Within ten years of the adoption of the *San Remo Manual*, it was 'widely accepted as being declaratory of the present law of naval warfare',[54] including in relation to the establishment of exclusion zones.

7.2.2 The Montreux Document and the International Code of Conduct in Practice

Widely cited and referenced by States, intergovernmental and non-governmental organizations, and private entities since its adoption, the Montreux Document has had considerable impact on State practice. It has been cited by States in and before UN bodies[55] and by UN bodies

54 Wolff Heintschel von Heinegg, 'Maritime Warfare', in Andrew Clapham and Paola Gaeta (eds), *The Oxford Handbook of International Law in Armed Conflict* (Oxford University Press, 2014), 146.

55 See Permanent Mission of Switzerland to the United Nations, *Note Verbale Dated 7 June 2012 from the Permanent Mission of Switzerland to the United Nations Addressed to the Secretary-General of the United Nations*, 202/12 SXN/ULN (7 June 2012); UN General Assembly and Security Council, *Letter Dated 2 October 2008 from the Permanent Representative of Switzerland to the United Nations Addressed to the Secretary-General*, UN Doc A/63/467–S/2008/636 (6 October 2008); UN Committee on the Rights of the Child, *Consideration of Reports Submitted by States Parties Under Article 8 of the Optional Protocol to the Convention on the Rights of Child on Involvement of Children in Armed Conflict: Initial Reports of States Parties Due in 2008 – Slovakia [30 October 2009]*, UN Doc CRC/C/OPAC/SVK/1 (14 June 2011), para 105; UN Security Council, 'Better Control of Borders, Private Security Firms Key to Stopping "Guns for Hire", Speakers Say at Security Council Debate on Mercenary Activities in Africa', UN Meetings Coverage and Press Releases, Security Council, 8456th Meeting, UN Doc SC/13688 (4 February 2019), https://press.un.org/en/2019/sc13688.doc.htm; United Nations, 'In Presidential Statement, Security Council Reaffirms Commitment to Protection of Civilians in Armed Conflict, Adopts Updated Aide Memoire on Issue', UN Meetings Coverage and Press Releases, Security Council, 6427th Meeting, UN Doc SC/10089 (22 November 2010), www.un.org/unispal/document/auto-insert-207387/; United Nations, 'Despite Progress, Civilians Continue to Bear Brunt of Conflict, Says Under-Secretary-General in Briefing to Security Council', UN Meetings Coverage and Press Releases, Security Council, 6151st Meeting, UN Doc SC/9692 (26 June 2009), https://press.un.org/en/2009/sc9692.doc.htm; UN General Assembly, *Note Verbale Dated 26 July 2016 from the Permanent Mission of Croatia to the United Nations Addressed to the President of the General Assembly*, UN Doc A/71/225 (28 July 2016); UN Committee against Torture and Other Cruel, Inhuman or Degrading Treatment or Punishment, *List of Issues in Connection with the Consideration of the Fifth Periodic Report of the United Kingdom of Great Britain and Northern Ireland, Adopted by the Committee at Its Forty-ninth Session (29 October–23 November 2012)*, UN Doc CAT/C/GBR/Q/5/Add.1 (2 May 2013); UN General Assembly Sixth Committee, *Summary Record of the 15th Meeting*, UN Doc A/C.6/69/SR.15 (2 December 2014); UN Committee on the Rights of the Child, *Consideration of Reports Submitted by States Parties Under Article 8(1) of the Optional Protocol to the Convention on the Rights of the Child on the Involvement of Children in Armed Conflict: Initial Reports of States Parties Due in 2008 – Slovakia*, UN Doc CRC/C/OPAC/SVK/1 (13 May 2011); UN Security Council, *Meeting Records, 6151st Meeting*, Statement by the Permanent Representative of Mexico, UN Doc S/PV.6151 (26 June 2009), 20; UN Security Council, *Comments by Poland, France, Germany, the United Kingdom, and South Africa*, UN Doc S/PV.8456 (4 February 2019); UN General Assembly, *Use of Mercenaries as a Means of Violating Human*

themselves,[56] as well as in the European Parliament,[57] the European Commission for Democracy through Law,[58] the Permanent Council of the

---

Rights and Impeding the Exercise of the Right of Peoples to Self-Determination: Note by the Secretary-General, UN Doc A/77/268 (4 August 2022); International Law Commission, *Report of the International Law Commission on the Work of Its Seventy-third Session (18 April–3 June and 4 July–5 August 2022)*, UN Doc A/77/10 (2022), Principle 10, para 9; UN Security Council, *Conflict-Related Sexual Violence: Report of the Secretary-General*, UN Doc S/2023/413 (22 June 2023), para 91(e).

56 See the following from the UN Human Rights Council, *Report of the Open-Ended Intergovernmental Working Group to Consider the Possibility of Elaborating an International Regulatory Framework on the Regulation, Monitoring and Oversight of the Activities of Private Military and Security Companies on Its Second Session*, UN Doc A/HRC/22/41 (24 December 2012), *Report of the Open-Ended Intergovernmental Working Group to Consider the Possibility of Elaborating an International Regulatory Framework on the Regulation, Monitoring and Oversight of the Activities of Private Military and Security Companies on Its Fourth Session*, UN Doc A/HRC/30/47 (9 July 2015); *Promotion and Protection of All Human Rights, Civil, Political, Economic, Social and Cultural Rights, Including the Right to Development: Report of the Working Group on the Use of Mercenaries as a Means of Violating Human Rights and Impeding the Exercise of the Right of Peoples to Self-Determination*, UN Doc A/HRC/10/14 (21 January 2009); *Report of the Working Group on the Use of Mercenaries as a Means of Violating Human Rights and Impeding the Exercise of the Right of Peoples to Self-Determination*, UN Doc A/HRC/15/25 (5 July 2010); See also International Law Commission, *Second Report on Protection of the Environment in Relation to Armed Conflicts by Marja Lehto, Special Rapporteur*, Seventy-first Session, 29 April–7 June 2019 and 8 July–9 August 2019, UN Doc A/CN.4/728 (27 March 2019); UN Office on Drugs and Crime, *State Regulation Concerning Civilian Private Security Services and Their Contribution to Crime Prevention and Security Safety* (UNODC, 2014), 83–84.

There have also been numerous discussions of the Montreux Document in the Third and Sixth Committees. (e.g. United Nations, 'Flouting International Law, Racism Pervades All Countries, Third Committee Hears at Start of Debate', UN Meetings Coverage and Press Releases, General Assembly, Sixty-ninth Session, 37th & 38th Meetings, UN Doc GA/SHC/4115 (3 November 2014), https://press.un.org/en/2014/gashc4115.doc.htm; United Nations, 'Responsibility of States to Ensure Protection of Diplomatic Personnel, Premises Is Reviewed by Assembly's Legal Committee', UN Meetings Coverage and Press Releases, General Assembly, Sixty-fifth General Assembly, Sixth Committee, 13th & 14th Meetings, UN Doc GA/L/3394, (18 October 2010), https://press.un.org/en/2010/gal3394.doc.htm.

57 European Parliament, *Resolution of 21 January 2016 on Estonian and UK Seamen under detention in India* (2016/2522(RSP)), P8_TA(2016)0022, para 6; European Parliament, *Resolution of 8 October 2013 on Corruption in the public and private sectors: the impact on human rights in third countries* (2013/2074(INI)), P7_TA(2013)0394, preamble and para 44; European Parliament, 'Joint answer given by High Representative/Vice-President Ashton on behalf of the Commission', 2 August 2012, *Official Journal of the European Union*, vol 56, C 262E/132 (11 September 2013); European Parliament, Committee of Foreign Affairs, *Draft Report on Human Rights Concerns in Private Military and Security Companies' Operations Affecting Third Countries* (2018/2154(INI), 17 July 2018); European Parliament, *Resolution of 25 November 2021 on the human rights violations by private military and security companies, particularly the Wagner Group* (2021/2982(RSP)), preamble and para c.

58 European Commission for Democracy through Law (Venice Commission), *Report on Private Military and Security Firms and Erosion of the State Monopoly on the Use of Force* (Study No 531/2009, 29 June 2009), 3, 5–8, 12–14, 19; and *2009 Annual Activity Report* (Council of Europe, 2010), 40–41.

Organization of American States,[59] and official Australian,[60] Canadian,[61] UK,[62] and US[63] governmental and parliamentary documentation.

More broadly, research undertaken in 2017 indicates the positive impact of the Montreux Document on the regulation of PMSCs.[64] Most States that have signed on have since passed new domestic legislation or amended existing legislation to regulate the activities of PMSCs.[65]

Even non-Montreux States and organizations (including the United Nations and the Economic Community of West African States) and private entities have incorporated many of Montreux's good practice recommendations.[66] So have private entities, such as ASIS International (one of the world's largest peak bodies for security professionals), which incorporated Montreux into its management system standards.)[67]

59 Permanent Council of the Organization of American States, Committee on Juridical and Political Affairs, *Final Report: Special Meeting on International Humanitarian Law [AG/RES. 2507 (XXXIX-O/09)]* (29 January 2010).

60 Australia, *Parliamentary Debates* (Hansard), Senate, 18 October 2010, Foreign Affairs, Defence and Trade Legislation Committee, Estimates (Supplementary Budget Estimates), 44.

61 Canada, *Parliamentary Debates* (Hansard), House of Commons, 6 May 2009, vol 144, no 052, 3148 (Oral Questions, Response of Peter MacKay, Minister of National Defence and Minister of the Atlantic Gateway); Canada, *Parliamentary Debates* (Hansard), House of Commons, 7 February 2011, vol 145, no 125, 7789 (Oral Questions, Response of Lawrence Cannon, Minister for Foreign Affairs); Canada, *Parliamentary Debates* (Hansard), House of Commons, 9 February 2011, vol 145, no 127, 7940 (Oral Questions, Response of Lawrence Cannon, Minister for Foreign Affairs).

62 See United Kingdom Secretary of State, Ministry of Defence, Letter to Rt Hon James Arbuthnot MP, on the Ministry's approach toward private security companies (12 May 2014), www.parliament.uk/documents/commons-committees/defence/140512-SoS-to-Chair-re-Private-Security-Companies.pdf; United Kingdom, *Parliamentary Debates* (Hansard), House of Lords, 30 October 2012, vol 740, col 495.

63 Including that the Afghan Public Protection Force 'adhere to the Afghan Public Protection Force Code of Conduct and applicable international standards, such as the Montreux Document, and the International Code of Conduct for private security service providers', outlined in sec 1535(c)(3)(iii), National Defense Authorization Act for Fiscal Year 2013, Pub L No 112–239. See also Congressional Research Service (United States), *The Department of Defense's Use of Private Security Contractors in Afghanistan and Iraq: Background, Analysis, and Options for Congress* (CRS Report No R40835, updated 13 May 2011); Jennifer K Elsea, *Private Security Contractors in Iraq and Afghanistan: Legal Issues* (CRS Report No R40991, 7 January 2010).

64 Geneva Centre for the Democratic Control of Armed Forces, *The Montreux Document: A Mapping Study on Outreach and Implementation* (DCAF, 2017). See also Benjamin S Buckland and Anna Marie Burdzy, *Progress and Opportunities: Challenges and Recommendations for Montreux Document Participants* (2nd ed, Geneva Centre for the Democratic Control of Armed Forces, 2015), www.montreuxdocument.org/pdf/Progress-and-Opportunities-Challenges-and-Recommendations-for-Montreux-Document-Participants-2nd-edition.pdf.

65 *The Montreux Document*, 12.

66 *The Montreux Document*, 22.

67 ASIS International, *ANSI/ASIS PSC.1–2012: Management System for Quality of Private Security Company Operations – Requirements with Guidance* (5 March 2012); ASIS International, *PSC.4–2013: Quality Assurance and Security Management for Private Security Companies Operating at Sea – Guidance* (29 January 2013).

Officially adopted on 9 November 2010 with 58 private security companies[68] as signatories,[69] the International Code of Conduct for Private Security Service Providers would encompass over 700 companies by 2013.[70] The International Code of Conduct Association (the oversight mechanism for the Code) also boasts extensive State and industry engagement. In 2014, it had 88 industry members[71] but grew to 132 members by 2023.[72]

The Code also has been cited in UN bodies,[73] in UN practice,[74] and in the practice of States.[75]

In an appearance before the International Maritime Organization, Singapore and the Philippines cited the Code as part of their call for the need for guidance regarding the use of PMSCs in anti-piracy operations.[76]

68 The companies are listed in David A Wallace, 'International Code of Conduct for Private Security Service Providers' (2011) 50 *International Legal Materials* 89, 103–104.

69 See Geneva Academy, *The International Code of Conduct for Private Security Service Providers* (Academy Briefing No 4, August 2013).

70 See Federal Council (Switzerland), 'International Code of Conduct for Private Security Service Providers – Consensus on Oversight Mechanism' (22 February 2013), www.admin.ch/gov/en/start/dokumentation/medienmitteilungen.msg-id-47889.html.

71 International Code of Conduct Association, *Annual Report 2013–2014* (ICoCA, 2014), 4.

72 International Code of Conduct Association, 'Members', https://icoca.ch/membership/.

73 UN Human Rights Council, *Summary of the Third Session of the Open-Ended Intergovernmental Working Group to Consider the Possibility of Elaborating an International Regulatory Framework on the Regulation, Monitoring and Oversight of the Activities of Private Military and Security Companies*, UN Doc A/HRC/WG.10/3/2 (2 September 2014); UN HRC, *Report of the Open-Ended Intergovernmental Working Group to Consider the Possibility of Elaborating an International Regulatory Framework on the Regulation, Monitoring and Oversight of the Activities of Private Military and Security Companies on Its Second Session*, UN Doc A/HRC/22/41 (24 December 2012); UN Human Rights Council, *Summary of the First Session of the Open-Ended Intergovernmental Working Group to Consider the Possibility of Elaborating an International Regulatory Framework on the Regulation, Monitoring and Oversight of the Activities of Private Military and Security Companies*, UN Doc A/HRC/WG.10/1/4 (22 November 2011); UN HRC, *Report of the Open-Ended Intergovernmental Working Group to Consider the Possibility of Elaborating an International Regulatory Framework on the Regulation, Monitoring and Oversight of the Activities of Private Military and Security Companies on Its Fourth Session*, UN Doc A/HRC/30/47 (9 July 2015); International Law Commission, *Summary Record of the 3275th Meeting*, UN Doc A/CN.4/SR.3275 (22 September 2015); UN Security Council, 'Better Control of Borders' (comments by France).

74 UN Department of Safety and Security, *United Nations Security Management System: Security Policy Manual* (2011), 95; UN Human Rights Council, *Report of the Working Group on the Use of Mercenaries as a Means of Violating Human Rights and Impeding the Exercise of the Right of Peoples to Self-Determination: Mission to Ghana (8 to 15 December 2017)*, UN Doc A/HRC/39/49/Add.1 (7 December 2018).

75 UN General Assembly, *Note Verbale Dated 26 October 2016 from the Permanent Mission of the United States of America to the United Nations Addressed to the President of the General Assembly*, UN Doc A/71/585 (31 October 2016); UN Human Rights Committee, *Consideration of Reports Submitted by States Parties Under Article 40 of the Covenant, Fourth Periodic Report: United States of America [30 December 2011]*, UN Doc CCPR/C/USA/4 (22 May 2012).

76 International Maritime Organization, Maritime Safety Committee, *Piracy and Armed Robbery Against Ships: Development of Guidance for the Industry on the Employment of Private Armed*

7.2.3 The ICRC CIHL Study in Practice

The ICRC CIHL study has been cited in UN bodies;[77] in parliamentary debates prior to legislative reform in Australia;[78] in courts in Canada,[79] Israel,[80] the Philippines,[81] the United Kingdom,[82] and the United States;[83] and in the European Court of Human Rights,[84] the Inter-American Court of Human Rights,[85]

Security Service Providers to Deter and Counter Piracy Against Ships, Submitted by the Philippines, Singapore, BIMCO and ICS, MSC/89/18/5 (8 March 2011).

77 International Law Commission, *Second Report on Protection of the Environment in Relation to Armed Conflicts by Marja Lehto, Special Rapporteur*, Seventy-first Session, 29 April–7 June 2019 and 8 July–9 August 2019, UN Doc A/CN.4/728 (27 March 2019), 12, 24, 26–28, 74–76; UN Human Rights Council, *Implementation of General Assembly Resolution 60/251 of 15 March 2006 Entitled 'Human Rights Council': Report of the Commission of Inquiry on Lebanon Pursuant to Human Rights Council Resolution S-2/1*, UN Doc A/HRC/3/2 (23 November 2006), 24; International Law Commission, *Report of the International Law Commission on the Work of Its Seventy-first Session (29 April–7 June and 8 July–9 August 2019)*, UN Doc A/74/10 (2019), 73–74; International Law Commission, *Report of the International Law Commission on the Work of Its Sixty-eighth Session (2 May–10 June and 4 July–12 August 2016)*, Supplement No 10, UN Doc A/71/10 (2024), 87, 90, 161–162, 323–324; International Commission of Inquiry on Darfur, *Report to the United Nations Secretary-General Pursuant to Security Council Resolution 1564 of 18 September 2004* (25 January 2005), www2.ohchr.org/english/darfur.htm.

78 Crimes Legislation Amendment (Powers, Offences and Other Measures) Bill 2015, *Bills Digest* No 1 of 2015–16 (5 August 2015), 14; Parliamentary Joint Committee on Human Rights, *Human Rights Scrutiny Report: Twenty-second Report of the 44th Parliament* (13 May 2015), 141 (Counter-Terrorism Legislation Amendment Bill (No 1) 2014); Criminal Code Amendment (War Crimes) Bill 2016, *Bills Digest* No 43 of 2016–17 (23 November 2016), 6–7.

79 *R v Y (N)* 2008 CarswellOnt 3032 (2008) 77 WCB (2d) 686, 8–10.

80 *Public Committee Against Torture v Government*, HCJ 769/02 (14 December 2016), para 30; *Jaber Al-Bassiouni Ahmed v Prime Minister and Minister of Defence*, HCJ 9132/07 (27 January 2008), para 14.

81 *Lagman v Medialdea* [2017] 812 Phil Rep 179 (4 July), 657.

82 *Mohammed v Ministry of Defence* [2017] AC 649, 761–767, 778–780, 794–796; *Al-Waheed v Ministry of Defence* [2017] AC 821; *Mohammed v Ministry of Defence* [2014] EWHC 1369 (QB), para 260; *R v Gul* [2012] EWCA Crim 280, para 30; *KS (Anonymity Order Made) v Secretary of State for the Home Department* [2014] UKUT 00552 (IAC), para 2.

83 *Hamdan v Rumsfeld* [2006] 548 US 557.

84 *Sargsyan v Azerbaijan* [2017] 64 EHRR 4, 225, 260; *Korbely v Hungary* [2010] 50 EHRR 48, 1221–1222; *Muršić v Croatia* [2017] 65 EHRR 1, 77; *Marguš v Croatia* [2016] 62 EHRR 17, 575; *Chiragov v Armenia* [2016] 63 EHRR 9, 427; *Mocanu v Romania* [2015] 60 EHRR 19, 900; *Milanković v Croatia* (Application no 33351/20), Judgment (20 January 2022), paras 35–36; *Hanan v Germany* (Application no 4871/16), Judgment (16 February 2021), para 80.

85 *Massacres of El Mozote and Nearby Places v El Salvador*, Judgment (Merits, Reparations and Costs), Series C No 252 (25 October 2012), para 141; *Rochac Herandández v El Salvador*, Judgment (Merits, Reparations and Costs), Series C No 285 (14 October 2014), para 109; *Santo Domingo Massacre v Colombia*, Judgment (Preliminary Objections, Merits and Reparations), Series C No 259 (30 November 2012), para 187; *Vásquez Durand v Ecuador*, Judgment (Preliminary Objections, Merits, Reparations and Costs), Series C No 332 (15 February 2017); *Afro-descendant Communities Displaced from the Cacarica River Basin (Operation Genesis) v Colombia*, Judgment (Preliminary Objections, Merits, Reparations and Costs), Series C No 270 (20 November 2013), para 349.

the ICJ,[86] the ICC,[87] the ICTY,[88] the Special Court for Sierra Leone,[89] the Ethiopia-Eritrea Claims Commission,[90] and the Kosovo Specialist Chambers.[91] It is noteworthy that the study has been so widely embraced in practice as its entire purpose was determining whether specific provisions in the treaty

86 Public sitting held on Tuesday 7 March 2017, at 10 am, at the Peace Palace, President Abraham presiding, *Application of the International Convention for the Suppression of the Financing of Terrorism and of the International Convention on the Elimination of All Forms of Racial Discrimination (Ukraine v Russian Federation)*, ICJ, Verbatim Record 2017/2, 25–26; *Jurisdictional Immunities of the State (Germany v Italy: Greece intervening)*, Judgment, 2012 ICJ Rep 99 (3 February), Dissenting Opinion of Judge Cançado Trindade, paras 116, 246; *Questions Relating to the Obligation to Prosecute or Extradite (Belgium v Senegal)*, Judgment, 2012 ICJ Rep 422 (20 July), Separate Opinion of Judge Cançado Trindade, para 134; Public sitting held on Monday 25 April 2005, at 3 pm, at the Peace Palace, President Shi presiding, *Armed Activities on the Territory of the Congo (Democratic Republic of the Congo v Uganda)*, ICJ, Verbatim Record, 2005/13, 31–32.

87 *Situation in the Democratic Republic of the Congo, Prosecutor v Bosco Ntaganda*, Pre-Trial Chamber II, ICC-01/04-02/06, Public Redacted Version of Prosecution's submissions on issues that were raised during the confirmation of charges hearing, 7 March 2014, ICC-01/04-02/06-276-Conf, ICC-01/04-02/06-276-Red (24 March 2014), 75; *Situation in Darfur, Sudan, Prosecutor v Bahar Idriss Abu Garda*, Pre-Trial Chamber I, Decision on the Confirmation of Charges (8 February 2010), ICC-02/05-02/09 (8 February 2010), 40; *Situation in the Central African Republic, Prosecutor v Jean-Pierre Bemba Gombo*, Trial Chamber III, Public Redacted Version of 'Prosecution's Response to the Defence Closing Brief', 15 September 2014, ICC-01/05-01/08-3141-Conf, ICC-01/05-01/08 (22 April 2016), 35–36; *Situation in the Democratic Republic of Congo, Prosecutor v Germain Katanga*, Trial Chamber II, United Nations Joint Submission on Reparations, ICC-01/04-01/07 (14 May 2015); *Situation in the Democratic Republic of the Congo, Prosecutor v Bosco Ntaganda*, Appeals Chamber, Public Redacted Version of judgment on the Appeals of Mr Bosco Ntaganda and the Prosecutor against the Decision of Trial Chamber VI of 8 July 2019 entitled 'Judgment', ICC-01/04-02/06/2666-Red (30 March 2021), para 549.

88 *Prosecutor v Enver Hadzihasanovic*, Decision on Joint Defence Interlocutory Appeal of Trial Chamber Decision on Rule 98 *BIS* Motions for Acquittal, Appeals Chamber, Case No IT-01–47-AR73.3 (11 March 2005); *Prosecutor v Milomir Stakic*, Judgment, Appeals Chamber, Case No IT-97–24-A (22 March 2006); *Prosecutor v Ljube Boškoski*, Judgment, Trial Chamber II, Case No IT-04–82-T (10 July 2008), 93; *Prosecutor v Naser Orić*, Appeals Chamber, Judgment, IT-03–68-A (3 July 2008), 83–84; *Prosecutor v Mitar Rašević*, Referral Bench, Decision on Referral of Case under Rule 11 *BIS*, Case No IT-97–25/1-PT (8 July 2005), 23; *Prosecutor v Enver Hadžihasanović*, Trial Chamber, Judgment, Case No IT-01–47-T (15 March 2006), 69–70.

89 *Prosecutor v Sam Hinga Norman*, Decision on Preliminary Motion based on Lack of Jurisdiction (Child Recruitment), Special Court for Sierra Leone, Appeals Chamber, Case No SCSL-2004–14-AR72(E) (31 May 2004).

90 Eritrea-Ethiopia Claims Commission, Partial Award, *Prisoners of War – Eritrea's Claim 17* (1 July 2003), para 41; Eritrea-Ethiopia Claims Commission, Partial Award, *Prisoners of War – Ethiopia's Claim 4*, para 32 (concerning the Geneva Conventions); Eritrea-Ethiopia Claims Commission, Partial Award, *Central Front – Eritrea's Claims 2, 4, 6, 7, 8 & 22* (28 April 2004), para 23; Eritrea-Ethiopia Claims Commission, Partial Award, *Central Front – Ethiopia's Claim 2* (28 April 2004), para 17; Eritrea-Ethiopia Claims Commission, Partial Award, *Western Front, Aerial Bombardment and Related Claims – Eritrea's Claims 1, 3, 5, 9–13, 14, 21, 25 & 26* (19 December 2005), paras 95, 104–105.

91 *Prosecutor v Hashim Thaçi*, Kosovo Specialist Chambers, Case No KSC-BC2020–05-F00026-RED, Public Redacted Version of Decision on the Confirmation of the Indictment against Hashum Thaçi, Kadri Veseli, Rexhep Selimi and Jakup Krasniqi (Basic Court Chamber) (26 October 2020); *Prosecutor v Pjetër Shala*, Kosovo Specialist Chambers, Case No

law of armed conflict – namely, API[92] and Additional Protocol II (APII)[93] – had achieved customary status, such that the rules were binding on all States, even those States that had not ratified the treaties in question. Neither API nor APII has achieved universal ratification by States. Yet one of the key findings of the ICRC study was that many, if not most, of the substantive provisions of the Protocols have achieved customary status.

While the study's findings were contentious at the time of publication,[94] the States (even those, such as Israel and the United States, not party to the Additional Protocols) have since come to accept the conclusions and to employ them in their own State practice as evidence of the customary status of many of the Protocols.

7.3 What Makes a Successful Non-Binding Instrument?

Having evaluated successful examples of soft law instruments, we must now ask additional questions. *Why* have these particular instruments been adopted by States? And *why* have they been successful while other comparable instruments have not? (For instance, contrast the *San Remo Manual* with the *Manual on International Law Applicable to Air and Missile Warfare*.[95])[96]

A more detailed analysis indicates that the relative success of a soft law instrument was highly dependent on several key factors:

1. The instrument should have a high level of State involvement, particularly the involvement of a highly representative and geographically diverse group of multiple States, and should include those with specific subject-matter interest and expertise in the area under examination. (For

---

KSC-BC-2020-04/F00007/RED/1, Public Redacted Version of the Decision on the Confirmation of the Indictment against Pjetër Shala (Basic Court Chamber) (12 June 2020).

92 Protocol Additional to the Geneva Conventions of 12 August 1949, and Relating to the Protection of Victims of International Armed Conflicts, opened for signature 8 June 1977, entered into force 7 December 1978, 1125 UNTS 3 (API).

93 Protocol Additional to the Geneva Conventions of 12 August 1949, and Relating to the Protection of Victims of Non-International Armed Conflicts, opened for signature 8 June 1977, entered into force 7 December 1978, 1125 UNTS 609 (APII).

94 See Claude C Emanuelli, 'Comments on the ICRC Study on Customary International Humanitarian Law' (2007) 44 *Canadian Yearbook of International Law* 437; Daniel Bethlehem, 'The Methodological Framework of the Study', in Elizabeth Wilmshurst and Susan Breau (eds), *Perspectives on the ICRC Study on Customary International Humanitarian Law* (Cambridge University Press, 2007); John Bellinger and William Haynes, Letter to the President of the ICRC, excerpted in 'United States Responds to ICRC Study on Customary International Law' (2007) 101 *American Journal of International Law* 639, 640.

95 Program on Humanitarian Policy and Conflict Research at Harvard University, *Manual on International Law Applicable to Air and Missile Warfare* (HPCR, 2009).

96 See Crawford, *Non-Binding Norms*, 198–209.

example, an instrument regulating private military and security companies should involve States that have employed such companies and those whose territories have been occupied by them.)
Successful instruments have typically involved several States as the progenitors of the instrument from the outset (as with the Montreux Document) or States that were otherwise deeply involved in the creation of the instrument. In the absence of State involvement at the preliminary stages, successful soft law instruments have often involved highly regarded subject-matter experts or institutions that have recognized interests or expertise in the topic, such as the ICRC. (We see this with the ICRC CIHL study.)[97]

2. The drafting process should include diverse contributors in terms of expertise, geographical region, and legal tradition. Instruments that have been successful have largely drawn participants who meet the requirements of both subject-matter expertise and diversity in terms of geography (as with the ICRC CIHL study and the *San Remo Manual*). Instruments that have not been as successful in practice, such as the first iteration of the *Tallinn Manual*,[98] were criticized for, inter alia, selecting participants from only a limited number of jurisdictions, which led to a 'clear problem of representativeness'.[99]
3. The document should clearly distinguish between the *lex lata* and the *lex ferenda* of a given situation. A common criticism of some soft law instruments has been a propensity in those instruments to elide this clear distinction and present the *lex ferenda* as *lex lata* (for example, with the ICRC guidance on direct participation in hostilities).[100] Therefore, the closer the document in question hews to the accepted law (if, of course, a statement of the law is its stated aim) and clearly states *lex ferenda* as *lex ferenda*, the more likely it is to be accepted in practice.

97 Jean-Marie Henckaerts and Louise Doswald-Beck (eds), *Customary International Humanitarian Law* (Cambridge University Press, 2005). See Crawford, *Non-Binding Norms*, ch 8.

98 Michael N Schmitt (ed), *Tallinn Manual on the International Law Applicable to Cyber Warfare* (Cambridge University Press, 2013).

99 For other critiques of the *Tallinn Manual* 1.0, see further Dieter Fleck, 'Searching for International Rules Applicable to Cyber Warfare – A Critical First Assessment of the New *Tallinn Manual*' (2013) 18 *Journal of Conflict and Security Law* 331; Kristen Eichensehr, 'Review of *Tallinn Manual on the International Law Applicable to Cyber Warfare*' (2014) 108 *American Journal of International Law* 588.

100 W Hays Parks, 'Part IX of the ICRC "Direct Participation in Hostilities" Study: No Mandate, No Expertise, and Legally Incorrect' (2010) 42 *New York University Journal of International Law and Politics* 769; William Boothby, '"And for Such Time as": The Time Dimension to Direct Participation in Hostilities' (2010) 42 *New York University Journal of International Law and Politics* 741; Kenneth Watkin, 'Opportunity Lost: Organised Armed Groups and the ICRC "Direct Participation in Hostilities" Interpretive Guidance' (2010) 42 *New York University Journal of International Law and Politics* 641; Jann Kleffner, 'Section IX of the ICRC Interpretive Guidance on Direct Participation in Hostilities: The End of *Jus in Bello* Proportionality As We Know It?' (2012) 45 *Israel Law Review* 35.

Success for these instruments thus seems deeply connected to ideas of perceived reliability and legitimacy of either the origins, the participants, the process, or the outcome. Indeed, there is a wealth of literature that posits that laws are effective (and seen as effective) when they are perceived as 'legitimate' by their addressees and that this legitimacy serves to increase the degree of compliance with and respect for a particular law.[101] Legitimacy of origin, of process, of participants, and of outputs seems to correlate with increased respect for an instrument purporting to dictate behaviour.[102]

In this respect, successful soft law instruments in international humanitarian law seem to meet these criteria: they emanate from (or otherwise deeply involve) States or other entities vested (or quasi-vested) with lawmaking powers at the international law; they engage with subject-matter experts drawn from diverse and geographically and legally representative regions; and their outputs are soundly based on *lex lata*, with any findings that could be considered *lex ferenda* clearly noted as such.

7.4 A Non-Binding Instrument for NC3

Considering this, how to proceed in developing a NC3 code of conduct? We must remember the legitimization 'requirements' for the creation of successful non-binding instruments. Non-binding instruments that have failed or been less successful in practice are often those that did not commit to clear and unwavering origin, process, or output legitimacy.

101 See Thomas M Franck, 'The Power of Legitimacy and the Legitimacy of Power: International Law in an Age of Power Disequilibrium' (2006) 100 *American Journal of International Law* 88; Renate Mayntz, 'Legitimacy and Compliance in Transnational Governance' (*MPIfG Working Paper No 10/5*, Max Planck Institute for the Study of Societies, 2010), 12; Robert Baldwin, Cave, and Lodge, *Understanding Regulation: Theory, Strategy, and Practice* (2nd ed, Oxford University Press, 2012), 26–31; Ingo Take, 'Legitimacy in Global Governance: International, Transnational and Private Institutions Compared' (2012) 18 *Swiss Political Science Review* 220; Rüdiger Wolfrum, 'Legitimacy of International Law from a Legal Perspective: Some Introductory Considerations', in Rüdiger Wolfrum and Volker Röben (eds), *Legitimacy in International Law* (Springer, 2008); Daniel Bodansky, 'Legitimacy', in Daniel Bodansky, Jutta Brunnée, and Ellen Hey (eds), *The Oxford Handbook of International Environmental Law* (Oxford University Press, 2008); Thomas M Franck, *The Power of Legitimacy Among Nations* (Oxford University Press, 1990).

102 See Franck, *The Power of Legitimacy Among Nations*, 25, 50; Ian Hurd, 'Legitimacy and Authority in International Politics' (1999) 53 *International Organisation* 379, 387; Helen Keller, 'Codes of Conduct and Their Implementation: The Question of Legitimacy', in Rüdiger Wolfrum and Volker Röben (eds), *Legitimacy in International Law* (Springer, 2008), 256; Dominik Zaum, 'Legitimacy', in Jacob Katz Cogan, Ian Hurd, and Ian Johnstone (eds), *The Oxford Handbook of International Organizations* (Oxford University Press, 2016), 1110; Thomas Risse, 'Transnational Governance and Legitimacy', in Arthur Benz and Yannis Papadopoulos (eds), *Governance and Democracy: Comparing National, European and International Experiences* (Routledge, 2006), 183.

Firstly, an NC3 instrument should hew to processes that ensure origin legitimacy. The process that leads to the code should be spearheaded by a State, international, or intergovernmental organization with the perceived legitimacy and authority to steer such an endeavour; a nuclear weapons State would be an obvious choice, but a respected international or NGO with a particular interest in the area may be a reasonable choice also.

Any entity tasked with stewarding such a code should uphold process legitimacy at all stages and should maintain the highest level of transparency, consistency, and representativeness of process. For example, the process must have a clear mandate from the outset – that all participants are made aware of the parameters of the code and its aims and objectives: the adoption of a non-binding code of conduct for best practice in NC3. The transmittal of briefing documents, expert reports, and a draft code well in advance of any meetings would be an obvious step in achieving transparency and thus process legitimacy. The process should always follow the stated aims as outlined in the briefing documents and other materials; there should be no attempt to alter the parameters of the discussion or add new areas of regulation.

All interested parties and stakeholders – in particular, all declared nuclear States and any States under nuclear umbrellas – should be involved in the process of debating and adopting the document. There should also be an attempt to engage the participation of undeclared or aspirational nuclear States in the process. It would also be highly advantageous to include non-State NC3 experts, in an advisory capacity, in the drafting process. Such experts could include academics (such as security studies experts), former military personnel with training and expertise in NC3 (provided such personnel participate in a personal capacity and with the understanding that no classified or privileged information will be revealed), and other technical experts who have knowledge of how ideal NC3 systems should operate.

Finally, the document must adhere to the highest level of output legitimacy. The final document must be presented clearly as *lex ferenda*, non-binding, and recommended practice only. There should be no attempt on behalf of the drafters or participants to present recommended practice as *lex lata*, even if such practice could potentially be considered as the early signs of an emergent customary international law. Above all, the recommend practice should take full account that it is aiming to guide behaviour in an area of State security that is highly secretive and of existential significance to those States in question.

Any successful code would need to ensure that its outcomes are reasonable and achievable – that objectives can be reasonably implemented, that they are suitable to purpose, and that they meet the fundamental policy and strategic aims of any NC3 system. Additionally, any code would have to appropriately consider the differing platforms and capabilities of each of the nuclear States.

Given the noted reluctance of States to adopt new treaties governing the conduct of hostilities, a non-binding code of conduct would arguably present the best opportunity to set down basic international rules for what is best practice in NC3. Fortunately, there is precedent in this arena: the Hague Code of Conduct Against Ballistic Missile Proliferation (HCoC).

7.4.1 The Hague Code of Conduct Against Ballistic Missile Proliferation

Adopted in 2002 as the result of efforts 'to internationally regulate the area of ballistic missiles capable of carrying weapons of mass destruction',[103] the HCoC was the initiative of the partner States of the Missile Technology Control Regime (MTCR,)[104] a 1987 initiative of the G7 States aimed at addressing the 'increasing proliferation of nuclear weapons by addressing the most destabilizing delivery system for such weapons'.[105] The MTCR achieves these aims through a commitment to export controls on equipment, software, and technology; through regular partner meetings; and through dialogue and outreach.[106] Thirty-five States are MTCR partners, including the nuclear States of France, India, Russia, the United Kingdom, and the United States, as well as several States under NATO and US nuclear umbrellas. Together, the MTCR and the HCoC exist as:

> [the] only multilateral transparency and confidence building instrument concerning the spread of ballistic missiles.
>
> By subscribing to the HCoC, members voluntarily commit themselves politically to provide pre-launch notifications (PLNs) on ballistic missile and space-launch vehicle launches (SLVs) and test flights. Subscribing States also commit themselves to submit an annual declaration (AD) of their country's policies on ballistic missiles and space-launch vehicles.[107]

As of this writing, 145 States have subscribed to the HCoC,[108] including the nuclear States of France, India, Russia, the United Kingdom, and the United

103 Hague Code of Conduct Executive Secretariat, 'The Hague Code of Conduct Against Ballistic Missile Proliferation (HCoC)' (March 2024), www.hcoc.at/.

104 For the origins of the HCoC, see Vann H Van Diepen, 'Origins and Development of the Hague Code of Conduct' (*HCoC Research Papers*, No 11, October 2022), www.nonproliferation.eu/hcoc/wp-content/uploads/2022/10/Origins-of-the-Code.pdf.

105 Missile Technology Control Regime, 'Frequently Asked Questions: 4. What Is the Purpose of the MTCR?', www.mtcr.info/en/faq. See also US Department of State, 'Missile Technology Control Regime (MTCR) Frequently Asked Questions: Fact Sheet' (2025), www.state.gov/bureau-of-international-security-and-nonproliferation/releases/2025/01/missile-technology-control-regime-mtcr-frequently-asked-questions.

106 Missile Technology Control Regime, *Equipment, Software and Technology Annex*, MTCR/TEM/2024/Annex (14 March 2024), www.mtcr.info/en/mtcr-annex.

107 Hague Code of Conduct Executive Secretariat, 'The Hague Code of Conduct Against Ballistic Missile Proliferation' (HCoC).

108 Hague Code of Conduct Executive Secretariat, 'List of HCoC Subscribing States' (January 2024), www.hcoc.at/subscribing-states/list-of-hcoc-subscribing-states.html.

States. As with the MTCR, the HCoC monitors compliance through regular meetings, information exchange, and voluntary reporting mechanisms, including providing pre-launch notifications on:

> ballistic missile and space-launch vehicle launches (SLVs) and test flights via the 'Restricted Website'. Subscribing States also commit themselves to submit an annual declaration (AD) of their country's policies on ballistic missiles and space-launch vehicles, including information on the number and generic class of ballistic missiles and space launch vehicles launched during the preceding year.[109]

The HCoC has been welcomed in State practice through endorsement in[110] and at the United Nations,[111] by the European Union,[112] in the practice of

109 Hague Code of Conduct Executive Secretariat, 'Frequently Asked Questions About HCoC' (March 2024), www.hcoc.at/what-is-hcoc/frequently-asked-questions.html.

110 Norway, Permanent Mission to the United Nations in New York, 'Statement by Permanent Representative Ambassador Merete Fjeld Brattested in the General Debate of the First Committee' (3 October 2023), www.norway.no/en/missions/un/statements/general-assembly-plenary/2023/statement-in-the-general-debate/1c-opening-statement/; Permanent Mission of the Federated States of Micronesia to the United Nations, *Statement by the Micronesian Delegation*, 76th Session of the United Nations General Assembly, Agenda Item 124: Strengthening of the United Nations System (8 June 2022), https://unmission.fm/wp-content/uploads/2022/06/Micronesia-DPRK-item-124.pdf.

111 The UN General Assembly has passed a supporting resolution regarding the Hague Code of Conduct Against Ballistic Missile Proliferation biannually since 17 December 2004. The most recent was on 7 December 2022 (UN Doc A/RES/77/58). See also UN Committee on the Peaceful Uses of Outer Space, *Voluntary Implementation of the Guidelines for the Long-term Sustainability of Outer Space Activities: Report by Italy*, UN Doc A/AC.105/C.1/2023/CRP.11 (6 February 2023), B.5.

112 Council of the European Union, Council Decision (CFSP) 2023/124 of 17 January 2023 in support of the Hague Code of Conduct and ballistic missile non-proliferation in the framework of the implementation of the EU Strategy against Proliferation of Weapons of Mass Destruction; Council of the European Union, Council Decision 2012/423/CFSP of 23 July 2012 in support of ballistic missile non-proliferation in the framework of the implementation of the EU Strategy against Proliferation of Weapons of Mass Destruction and of the Council Common Position 2003/805/CFSP; Council of the European Union, 'Annual Progress Report on the Implementation of the European Union Strategy Against the Proliferation of Weapons of Mass Destruction (2019)', *Official Journal of the European Union*, 2020/C 341/01 (13 October 2020), paras 46–49.

NATO[113] and ASEAN,[114] and in the practice of States including Germany,[115] Japan,[116] Norway,[117] and the Republic of Korea.[118]

MTCR partners might therefore present themselves as viable sponsors for any code of conduct for NC3, having already achieved success with MTCR and HCoC. Adopting a best practice code on NC3 would seem a logical and reasonable next step. However, any process to negotiate an NC3 code of conduct would need a draft instrument to discuss and debate. Therefore, this study now turns to examine possible rules for an NC3 code of conduct, including short comments on why such rules would be beneficial.

113 The HCoC is mentioned as an Official Text of NATO (NATO, 'Official Texts', https://natolibguides.info/missiledefence/documents), as well as in NATO, *NATO Standard AJP–3.23: Allied Joint Doctrine for Countering Weapons of Mass Destruction in Military Operations* (September 2023), at Annex C, C11.

114 ASEAN, 'Chairman's Statement the Tenth Meeting of ASEAN Regional Forum' (2 May 2020), https://asean.org/speechandstatement/chairmans-statement-the-tenth-meeting-of-asean-regional-forum/.

115 German Bundestag, *Germany's Global Role in Nuclear Disarmament and Non-Proliferation* (WD 2–3000 – 044/18, 11 April 2018), para 3.4, www.bundestag.de/resource/blob/557668/d9de6462b82653652b18fbb914834e82/WD-2-044-18-pdf-data.pdf.

116 Ministry of Foreign Affairs, Japan, 'Diplomatic Bluebook 2023: Japanese Diplomacy and International Situation in 2022' (2023), fn 27, www.ec.emb-japan.go.jp/files/100406514.pdf. See also Kawaguchi, Yoriko, 'Speech by Minister for Foreign Affairs Yoriko Kawaguchi to the Conference on Disarmament' (4 September 2003), www.disarm.emb-japan.go.jp/Statements/030904CD.htm.

117 Norway, Ministry of Trade and Fisheries, 'Meld. St. 10 (2019–2020): Høytflyvende satellitter – jordnære formal, En strategi for norsk romvirksomhet' [Report to the Storting (2019–2020): High-flying Satellites – Earth-based Purposes, A Strategy for Norwegian Space Activities] (2019), ch 8, www.regjeringen.no/no/dokumenter/meld.-st.-10-20192020/id2682361/?ch=8.

118 Republic of Korea, '2010 Defence White Paper' (2011), 11, 103, 402, www.files.ethz.ch/isn/155720/South%20Korea%202010_eng-1.pdf.

8 A Code of Conduct for State NC3

This book concludes its substantive analysis by essentially coming full circle. Previous chapters have essayed the declared nuclear doctrines of the various nuclear weapons States, their known NC3 systems, and the international law governing the possession and use of nuclear weapons. From this survey, we have seen that there is a wealth of international law that governs how States may (or may not) possess and use nuclear weapons, but there is little in the way of specific international law rules dictating the contours of a State's NC3 architecture. Building on this, the previous chapter looked at whether the adoption of a non-binding instrument on NC3 could help address this gap and examined what common factors seem to be present in existing non-binding international instruments (specific to situations of armed conflict) that have had a high degree of success in shaping State behaviour.

The book now turns to apply this framework to the specific task of developing a code of conduct for NC3, to outline what is *lex lata*, *lex ferenda*, and best practice for a nuclear weapons State's NC3 architecture. It is worthwhile here to remember what NC3 systems are for and why they are necessary. As explored at the beginning of this book, NC3 systems are, in essence, 'the medium by which the use of nuclear weapons can enter into military operations'.[1] To that end, it is worthwhile revisiting the key requirements of NC3 systems. As Boothby and Heintschel von Heinegg point out, a central purpose of an NC3 system is to ensure that, if used, nuclear weapons are only ever launched subject to legitimate authority and, inter alia, to ensure that:

> the threat or use of nuclear weapons is an absolutely last resort; that every less violent alternative to their use is pursued; that the resort to nuclear weapons is indeed prevented; and that confusion, ambiguity, uncertainty,

1 Hans Born, 'National Governance of Nuclear Weapons: Opportunities and Constraints' (*Geneva Centre for the Democratic Control of Armed Forces (DCAF), Policy Paper*, No 15, 2007), 15, www.dcaf.ch/sites/default/files/publications/documents/PP15_Born.pdf.

DOI: 10.4324/9781003759294-8

mis-communication and any other factor that may lead to strategic misunderstanding is, as far as possible, prevented.[2]

Any State NC3 is necessarily informed by distinct but interrelated objectives – its legal obligations and its strategic and policy objectives. Any legal obligations borne by a State will assert an influence on that State's NC3 architecture. For example, obligations under nuclear weapon–free zone treaties and existing laws on the use of force, the conduct of hostilities, and international criminal law will necessarily shape how any State structures its NC3 and related policies and practices. State NC3 must ensure that all international law obligations are complied with, in particular with regard to when such weapons may be lawfully used, in the context of both the use of force in self-defence and an ongoing armed conflict. NC3 architecture should be structured on the understanding of the rules on State responsibility for internationally wrongful acts, as well as the understanding of any individual criminal responsibility that might result from the illegal use of nuclear weapons.

States also have policy and strategic aims relating to nuclear weapons that their NC3 architecture will necessarily address. Those policy and strategic objectives will likely find expression in more 'practical' ways – any NC3 infrastructure should be structured in such a way as to ensure that only lawful orders are carried out, that unlawful or unverifiable orders are not executed, and that all steps are taken to eliminate the possibility of accidental or unauthorized deployment. As noted by Ildo Hwang:

> When a legitimate decision is made to use a nuclear weapon, the weapon system must be delivered and used without error. On the other hand, there should never be any accidental or erroneous use of nuclear weapons in all the other illegitimate cases. The problem is that there could be a fundamental trade-off between these two policy goals. This concern, often described as the 'always/never dilemma', can be cited as reasons why each country has built and developed its own command and control with characteristics that slightly differentiate it from other countries.[3]

A robust NC3 system can meet these requirements by demonstrating the qualities of being tightly held, in exclusively civilian control, responsive to a highly centralized hierarchy, and with nuclear weapons physically protected

2 William H Boothby and Wolff Heintschel von Heinegg, *The Law on Nuclear Weapons: An International Commentary* (Edward Elgar, 2025), 393.

3 Ildo Hwang, 'North Korea's Nuclear Command and Control Estimate: Variables and Trends' (2021) 33 *Korean Journal of Defense Analysis* 617, 618.

from unauthorized assembly or detonation.[4] NC3 should be hardened against external incursion from bad faith actors of any stripe (such as cyberattackers). These practical requirements can be met through functional means, such as ensuring:

- accurate, unambiguous, and authenticated identification of the national command authority, producing accurate and authenticated firing messages, with attendant human verification systems;
- a system architecture within the national command authority with no single point of failure and no possibility of a firing message being generated by any entity other than a State's national command authority;
- a system that has multiple, preferably simultaneous, transmission paths for the conveyance of firing messages, in order to ensure that transmission is not blocked by physical or electronic means, along with mechanisms in place to counter physical or electronic threats to messaging; and
- a system capable of operating at full functionality even after a nuclear strike and surviving the physical and electromagnetic pulse (EMP) damage that a major nuclear strike creates.

Given this strategic, policy, and legal background, what rules should therefore comprise an NC3 code of conduct? Any proposed code should clearly indicate which rules are binding international legal obligations and which are recommended best practice, in light of the objectives of an NC3. Additionally, any NC3 code would ideally contain a list of short, straightforward rules that are both clear enough and flexible enough that they can be universally applied by relevant stakeholders. However, it is imperative that every rule is accompanied by more comprehensive and detailed commentary and explanation regarding *why* such a rule has been included and the specifics of how the rule should be implemented, including examples of possible situations to which the rule would apply, as well as additional reference to further documentation (such as treaty law) where needed.

With these objectives in mind, this chapter now turns to proposing such a code. The draft Code of Conduct for State NC3 is divided into two parts, Part I being rules relating to salient international law obligations and Part II being rules prescribing recommended best practice. The code is devised to outline the basic rule in one or two sentences, followed by more specific explanation and commentary on what a more detailed State NC3 would require to ensure the rule is properly implemented.[5]

4 Sébastien Miraglia, 'Deadly or Impotent? Nuclear Command and Control in Pakistan' (2013) 36 *Journal of Strategic Studies* 841.

5 See for more detail Boothby and Heintschel von Heinegg, *The Law on Nuclear Weapons*, ch 12 (on legal issues and NC3).

Part I – Legal Obligations

Rule 1: *All States are under an obligation to refrain from the threat or use of nuclear force contrary to the UN Charter and the customary international law prohibition on the threat or use of force.*

- Individual State NC3 doctrine, whether publicly available or classified, should outline each State's position on what amounts to a threat or use of nuclear force and what amounts to an armed attack, as well as what criteria it would consider determinative of the existence of a threat of force, a use of force, and/or an armed attack.
- State NC3 should clearly indicate whether the State in question believes it is legal to use force against an imminent armed attack, including, potentially, any definition of imminence adopted by the State.
- State NC3 should also note the requirements for acts in collective self-defence under the UN Charter, which must include a prior request for assistance and timely reporting to the UN Security Council.

Rule 2: *In the conduct of nuclear hostilities, all States are bound by the customary international law of armed conflict, as well as any law of armed conflict treaty obligations that bind each State. Additionally, States must observe any other international law treaty obligations binding upon them, whether bilateral or multilateral, including regarding nuclear weapon–free zones.*

- Any State NC3 must be drafted in compliance with that State's obligations under the law of armed conflict. As a starting point, it is recommended that any State NC3 should outline the parameters for the existence of an international armed conflict and a non-international armed conflict, as well as when such situations are deemed to have ended.
- Documentation accompanying State NC3 should clearly indicate in the guidance a statement of existing binding legal obligations, as well as what is considered non-binding but has nonetheless been adopted by the State as policy or best practice.
- Any NC3 documentation should make particular note of the rules that relate to those persons and objects specially protected under international law, including, inter alia, civilians, children, journalists, medical and religious personnel, specially protected objects and installations, protected persons or objects connected to the United Nations or the ICRC, cultural property, works and installations containing dangerous forces, objects indispensable for the survival of the civilian population, and the natural environment.
- NC3 documentation should also ensure that protected subjects and objects that are at risk from the effects of nuclear targeting (for instance, due to their proximity to pre-existing lawful military objectives) are documented

and considered in the course of pre-conflict targeting and in nuclear strike decision-making.

Rule 3: *In the conduct of nuclear hostilities, States should be particularly aware of obligations regarding distinction and proportionality in attack and the prohibition on indiscriminate attack, as well as any prohibitions on particular means or methods of attack.*

- State NC3 should include clear rules on the principle of distinction regarding persons and objects. State NC3 should outline clearly whether a State has a particular position on what kinds of acts would, during a time of armed conflict, render a civilian as directly participating in hostilities, such that they could be lawfully targeted under the law of armed conflict. In particular, States should ensure that any civilian personnel engaged in nuclear weapons operations on behalf of the State are made aware of the consequences of such participation – that is, they may be targeted for such participation during an armed conflict, and they may not be entitled to prisoner of war protections if captured.
- State NC3 should clearly outline how military objectives are defined, including their position on so-called dual use objects (for example, whether they accept the US position that war-sustaining or war-supporting industries are legitimate targets under the law of armed conflict).
- State NC3 should outline the kinds of attacks and/or circumstances that would render an attack prima facie indiscriminate.
- State NC3 should clearly state the rule on proportionality in attack.
- Any State NC3 mechanism should clearly set forth the precautionary measures that the State is bound to apply in targeting situations, including the obligation to take constant care and the obligation to take precautions in attack. NC3 documentation should clearly outline who is under an obligation to take constant care and when and what kinds of precautions in attack are necessary (for example, the provision of warnings). NC3 documentation should clearly spell out how and why targets are selected and how collateral damage and proportionality assessments are to be made, what provisions exist for the cancellation or suspension of nuclear attacks, and whether advance warnings of attack are to be given. The provision of rules of engagement (ROEs) and/or standard operating procedure (SOP) documentation to all persons involved in nuclear operations is recommended.
- State NC3 should clearly state rules on permissible and impermissible means and methods of attack.

Rule 4: *States have an obligation under international law to ensure that all nuclear weapons personnel are properly instructed in the law of armed conflict. Persons in command of nuclear weapons operations should be properly* *instructed in their obligations under the law of armed conflict and the law of command responsibility,*

- Persons responsible for carrying out nuclear strikes – commanders of SSBNs, pilots of nuclear launch aircraft, and those in charge of land-based launch facilities – must be secure in the knowledge that any order to launch transmitted to them is compliant with the law of armed conflict. Therefore, as appropriate to their station and rank, all personnel involved in nuclear launches must be trained in the law of armed conflict.
- Commanders involved in nuclear weapons operations should be properly instructed in the law of armed conflict, especially regarding command responsibility, as commanders may be responsible either for ordering an illegal attack or for failing to properly supervise or punish subordinates who carry out an illegal attack.
- To ensure that only legal orders are issued in times of armed conflict involving nuclear weapons, legal advisers trained in the law of armed conflict should be involved at all stages of the decision-making process that leads to a nuclear launch.

Rule 5: *All nuclear weapons operators should be made aware of their obligations under international criminal law, in particular the obligation to not obey manifestly illegal orders to strike using a nuclear weapon.*

- Under international criminal law, a subordinate has an obligation to disobey manifestly unlawful orders. Accordingly, there is no defence of obeying a superior order if the subordinate *should* have known the act ordered was manifestly unlawful.
- Orders to commit genocide or crimes against humanity are always considered manifestly unlawful.
- To ensure that nuclear weapons operators are aware of which kinds of orders are considered manifestly unlawful and for such operators to be certain that any orders they are given are lawful, training in the law of armed conflict should be provided to all nuclear weapons operators.

Rule 6: *Parties to an armed conflict, including those conflicts in which nuclear weapons are employed, must respect the neutrality of States not party to the armed conflict. Neutral States must ensure that they observe the law of neutrality, as failure to do so may result in the State being considered a party to the conflict and liable to targeting, including with nuclear weapons.*

- During a time of armed conflict, commanders and other high-ranking military and civilian personnel engaged in the overall strategy and execution of the armed conflict should be aware, where appropriate, of the law of neutrality and not engage in any acts that violate the rights of neutral States.

- Likewise, commanders and other high-ranking military and civilian personnel in neutral States should also be well versed in the law of neutrality and refrain from any acts that would result in the loss of neutral status (unless such acts are intentionally undertaken with the aim of becoming a party to the conflict).

Part II – Recommended/Best Practice

Part II of the draft Code of Conduct now turns to look at practical means and measures that nuclear States can take to ensure that NC3 systems operate at peak functionality. The rationale for the rules listed in this section is the same. Any nuclear weapons State's NC3 must be able to fulfil the strategic and policy aims of ensuring that nuclear weapons are used lawfully and without error and that there is no accidental, mistaken, or unlawful use. To facilitate this aim, there are various practical measures that should be implemented which will have the additional benefits of avoiding unnecessary escalation leading to the employment of nuclear weapons, as well as providing avenues for de-escalation. Likewise, facilitating the ultimate aims of NC3 can be achieved through ensuring that all avenues for communication between nuclear States remain secure and open, with due attention paid to ensuring that both physical and technological measures for protecting lines of communication are maintained in peacetime and in war. The rules outlined in this part of the Code are drawn from the known practice of nuclear States but are not found in law; rather, they are sensible policy based on acknowledged aims for NC3.

Rule 7: *All nuclear States should establish a legitimate and accountable national command authority for all nuclear forces, including implementing a two-person rule for all launch decisions and implementation steps in NC3 operations.*

- A legitimate and accountable national command should be established, tasked with ensuring that any and all nuclear decisions are made in accordance with existing international law.
- At a minimum, nuclear States should institute a two-person launch rule – meaning that at least two authorized delegated persons are required to agree to launch a nuclear weapon, whether in attack or defence. A two-person launch rule would assist in ensuring that an authorized launcher, if such a launcher 'went rogue' and decided to illegally use a nuclear weapon, would be physically and technically prevented from undertaking such an illegal launch, which could be an important security mechanism to prevent unauthorized usage of a weapon.

Rule 8: *Nuclear weapons should not be co-located with the nuclear weapons State's high command post or with any other early-warning interpretation sites or sensors.*

- To ensure the survivability of a State's NC3 mechanisms, States should ensure that nuclear weapons are not co-located either with the high command post or with any early-warning sensors or intelligence posts.
- In any armed conflict involving the use of nuclear weapons, it would be logical to assume that a primary target would be an adverse party's nuclear weapons stockpiles and launching sites. Were such weapons stored in the same locale as any pivotal NC3 infrastructure, the inevitable destruction of such infrastructure would necessarily diminish, if not outright destroy, the ability of the attacked State to detect incoming launches and to take measures to prevent or mitigate the impact of an attack (or, indeed, to accurately detect whether an attack is incoming at all). By not co-locating stockpiles and high command and/or early-warning infrastructure, States can ensure that vital NC3 infrastructure retains its survivability, even during a nuclear weapons exchange.

Rule 9: *NC3 communications should have dedicated systems that are not shared by conventional military systems.*

- NC3 communications should be conducted on dedicated systems, separate from conventional military systems. Military communications would be a primary target during any armed conflict (whether nuclear weapons were involved or not). To ensure the sanctity and survivability of the NC3, its communications systems should be kept distinct from conventional military systems.
- To prevent launches of nuclear weapons occurring due to incorrect or absent intelligence (as a result of degraded or destroyed communications systems), open and unfettered communication between nuclear weapons installations and nuclear high command is vital and should therefore not be at risk of targeting.

Rule 10: *All nuclear weapons States and nuclear-armed States should implement an open source, best practice, secure nuclear hotline (such as CATALINK)*[6] *with other nuclear-armed States.*

- Modern NC3 systems are often based on a mix of new and old technology, with some of the older systems vulnerable to disruption, degradation, or

6 From its developers: 'The CATALINK would rely on internationally driven open-source technology to maximize user integrity and trust. This system would exploit redundant transmission

destruction through cyber or other malicious modern attack mechanisms. If such NC3 systems do fail, the risk of unnecessary escalation of hostilities is clearly present.

- A resilient and secure communications system would be a critical element to assist in de-escalation and to keep lines of communication open. A system such as CATALINK or another hardened and secure hotline system would serve as an important backup should existing NC3 systems fail.

Rule 11: *In nuclear operations, to facilitate accurate and lawful decision-making and to enable de-escalation, national high command of a nuclear weapons State or nuclear-armed State should not be subject to attack or interference with a nuclear weapons State's national technical means.*

- Accurate, lawful, and timely communications and intelligence in relation to a nuclear State's conduct during an armed conflict are central to preventing unnecessary escalation of hostilities due to, for example, inaccurate intelligence. Given the centrality of communications systems to nuclear (and nuclear-dependent) States, no State engaged in conflict with nuclear States should target a nuclear State's national technical means.

Rule 12: *To ensure that nuclear States have accurate intelligence and sufficient time to process any intelligence on nuclear operations, countermeasures or other measures of reprisal should not be taken against a nuclear State's NC3.*

- In the conduct of hostilities, there are international laws that limit permissible objects of reprisal. There are no specific rules under international law that prohibit targeting a State's communications systems. However, accurate and timely communications and intelligence in relation to a nuclear State's conduct during an armed conflict are imperative to prevent unnecessary escalation due to inaccurate intelligence or unnecessarily shortened decision-making processes. To facilitate optimal decision-making, States engaged in conflict with nuclear States should not target a nuclear State's NC3 in reprisal or as a countermeasure. Precedent for a rule prohibiting the targeting of vital NC3 components can be found in pre-existing

---

capabilities to ensure that multiple parties could connect under extreme conditions, including loss of power and absence of cellular and internet connectivity. The endpoint devices would be designed for durability, availability, and ease of use, enabling parties to immediately connect with confidence amid crises. These devices will be built from the bottom-up through international collaborative efforts to ensure security, integrity, and resilience'. Nautilus Institute, Stanley Center for Peace and Security, and Technology for Global Security, *Last Chance: Communicating at the Nuclear Brink Scenarios and Solutions Workshop Synthesis Report* (14 May 2020), 2–3.

agreements between the United States and Russia and NATO, prohibiting and preventing attacks that interfere with a State's national technical means of verification.[7]

Rule 13: *To ensure the reliability of NC3 systems and to limit or prevent opportunities for illegal access to NC3, technologies essential to NC3 operations should not be shared or proliferated beyond those strictly required for NC3 systems.*

- Accurate information is pivotal in any nuclear operations. Given the potential vulnerability of certain legacy NC3 systems, the software and hardware that are unique to State NC3 should not be shared with other domestic non-NC3 systems or with any other State's NC3.
- Proliferation of the software and/or hardware beyond NC3 increases the risk that the software and/or hardware could be accessed and exploited for vulnerabilities by bad-faith actors, which, in turn, would undermine the reliability of any NC3 information.

Rule 14: *To avoid the risk of false positives, NC3 systems should always employ humans on the decision chain. Any decision to launch a nuclear weapon should not be left to artificial intelligence software.*

- AI systems are being increasingly integrated into State military operations and seem to offer the advantage of providing timely intelligence, free from the kinds of emotive and irrational decisions that humans can make in times of stress or crisis, such as impending or unfolding nuclear operations.
- However, AI systems have been shown to be imperfect and prone to programming bias. AI also lacks the very human element of situational awareness and the ability to engage in self-reflexive decision-making processes. For example, a State's NC3 could, whether through system error or external manipulation, register an incoming nuclear attack where no such attack exists (as with the famous Petrov incident in 1983, when Russian

7 Including the Strategic Arms Limitation Talks (SALT) I Treaty, 26 May 1972; the Intermediate Range Nuclear Forces (INF) Treaty, 8 December 1987, entered into force 1 June 1988; the Strategic Offensive Arms Reduction Treaty I, 31 July 1991, entered into force 5 December 1994 (START I); and the Treaty on Conventional Armed Forces in Europe, 19 November 1990, entered into force 9 November 1992. Non-interference measures are designed to preserve from attack or interference national technical means of verifying treaty compliance, including space-orbiting means. It would be a violation of the provisions on noninterference with national means of verification in the INF and START I treaties to use weapons against any early warning, imaging, or intelligence satellite and, by extension, against any ocean surveillance, signals, intelligence, or communications satellite.

early warning systems misidentified a meteorological phenomenon as an incoming US missile attack).[8] Ensuring that AI systems are never allowed to make nuclear launch decisions would contribute to ensuring that false positives are not actioned.

8 See further Zachary Kallenborn, 'Giving an AI Control of Nuclear Weapons: What Could Possibly Go Wrong?', *Bulletin of the Atomic Scientists* (1 February 2022), https://thebulletin.org/2022/02/giving-an-ai-control-of-nuclear-weapons-what-could-possibly-go-wrong/.

9 Concluding Comments

NC3 sits at the intersection of complex and occasionally contradictory strategic security and policy requirements, as well as attendant legal rights and obligations. For any nuclear State, a robust and dependable NC3 is therefore a necessity to ensure that the legal, policy, and strategic objectives for the State are consistently met. While the adoption of the TPNW is a welcome addition to the legal landscape, the current customary international law on nuclear weapons, as well as the law for those States not party to the TPNW, remains that nuclear weapons are not prima facie illegal. However, as explored in this study, the lack of a general prohibition on nuclear weapons does not create a legal landscape that leaves regulation of nuclear weapons solely to the discretion of the nuclear State. Such States must therefore ensure that their nuclear weapons are only ever used in extreme circumstances, and in strictest compliance with international law. Having clear guidelines on what is considered best practice in relation to NC3 architecture would go a considerable way to ensuring that nuclear weapons are only ever used as a last resort and in strict compliance with the applicable law and that accidental deployment of weapons never occurs.

DOI: 10.4324/9781003759294-9

References

Afina, Yasmin, and Tim Caughley, 'NATO and the Frameworks of Nuclear Non-proliferation and Disarmament: Challenges for the 10th NPT Review Conference' (*Research Paper, Chatham House*, 29 May 2020), www.chathamhouse.org/2020/05/nato-and-frameworks-nuclear-non-proliferation-and-disarmament/1-introduction.

Aguirre, Anthony, Emilia Javorsky, and Max Tegmark, '"Artificial Escalation": Imagining the Future of Nuclear Risk', *Bulletin of the Atomic Scientists* (17 July 2023), https://thebulletin.org/2023/07/artificial-escalation-imagining-the-future-of-nuclear-risk/.

Akande, Dapo, and Thomas Liefländer, 'Clarifying Necessity, Imminence, and Proportionality in the Law of Self-Defense' (2013) 107 *American Journal of International Law* 563.

Al Assad, Wael, 'The Quest for a WMD Free Zone in the Middle East: History, Lessons Learned, and the Way Forward' (2022) 5 *Journal for Peace and Nuclear Disarmament* 114.

ASEAN, 'Chairmans' Statement the Tenth Meeting of ASEAN Regional Forum' (2 May 2020), https://asean.org/speechandstatement/chairmans-statement-the-tenth-meeting-of-asean-regional-forum/.

ASIS International, *ANSI/ASIS PSC.1–2012: Management System for Quality of Private Security Company Operations – Requirements with Guidance* (5 March 2012).

ASIS International, *PSC.4–2013: Quality Assurance and Security Management for Private Security Companies Operating at Sea – Guidance* (29 January 2013).

Australia, *Parliamentary Debates* (Hansard), Senate, Foreign Affairs, Defence and Trade Legislation Committee, Estimates (Supplementary Budget Estimates, 18 October 2010).

Australia, Parliamentary Joint Committee on Human Rights, *Human Rights Scrutiny Report: Twenty-second Report of the 44th Parliament* (13 May 2015).

Australian Government Department of Defence, '2016 Defence White Paper' (2016), www.defence.gov.au/about/strategic-planning/defence-white-paper.

Australian Human Rights Commission, 'Using Artificial Intelligence to Make Decisions: Addressing the Problem of Algorithmic Bias' (2020), https://humanrights.gov.au/our-work/technology-and-human-rights/publications/technical-paper-addressing-algorithmic-bias.

Azad, Tahir Mahmood, and Karl Dewey, 'Assessing the Security of Pakistan's Nuclear Weapon Programme' (2023) 39 *Defense & Security Analysis* 123.
Baldwin, Robert, Martin Cave, and Martin Lodge, *Understanding Regulation: Theory, Strategy, and Practice* (2nd ed, Oxford University Press, 2012).
Bartels, Rogier, 'The Classification of Armed Conflicts by International Criminal Courts and Tribunals' (2020) 20 *International Criminal Law Review* 595.
Baxter, RR, 'International Law in "Her Infinite Variety"' (1980) 29 *International & Comparative Law Quarterly* 549.
Bellinger, John, and William Haynes, Letter to the President of the ICRC, excerpted in 'United States Responds to ICRC Study on Customary International Law' (2007) 101 *American Journal of International Law* 639.
Berman, Ayelet, and Ramses A Wessel, 'The International Legal Form and Status of Informal International Lawmaking Bodies: Consequences for Accountability', in Joost Pauwelyn, Ramses Wessel, and Jan Wouters (eds), *Informal International Lawmaking* (Oxford University Press, 2012).
Besson, Samantha, 'Sovereignty', *Max Planck Encyclopedia of Public International Law* (April 2011), https://opil.ouplaw.com/display/10.1093/law:epil/9780199231690/law-9780199231690-e1472?rskey=PEszU3&result=1&prd=MPIL.
Bethlehem, Daniel, 'The Methodological Framework of the Study', in Elizabeth Wilmshurst and Susan Breau (eds), *Perspectives on the ICRC Study on Customary International Humanitarian Law* (Cambridge University Press, 2007).
Bethlehem, Daniel, 'Principles Relevant to the Scope of a State's Right of Self-Defense Against an Imminent or Actual Armed Attack by Nonstate Actors' (2012) 106 *American Journal of International Law* 769.
Blay, Samuel KN, 'Territorial Integrity and Political Independence', *Max Planck Encyclopedia of Public International Law* (March 2010), https://opil.ouplaw.com/display/10.1093/law:epil/9780199231690/law-9780199231690-e1116.
Bodansky, Daniel, 'Legitimacy', in Daniel Bodansky, Jutta Brunnée, and Ellen Hey (eds), *The Oxford Handbook of International Environmental Law* (Oxford University Press, 2008).
Boothby, William, '"And for Such Time as": The Time Dimension to Direct Participation in Hostilities' (2010) 42 *New York University Journal of International Law and Politics* 741.
Boothby, William, *The Law of Targeting* (Oxford University Press, 2012).
Boothby, William H, 'Law, Targeting and Nuclear Operations' (*NAPSNet Special Reports*, 31 October 2019), https://nautilus.org/napsnet/napsnet-special-reports/law-targeting-and-nuclear-operations/.
Boothby, William H, and Wolff Heintschel von Heinegg, *The Law on Nuclear Weapons: An International Commentary* (Edward Elgar, 2025).
Boothby, William H, and Wolff Heintschel von Heinegg, *Nuclear Weapons Law: Where Are We Now?* (Cambridge University Press, 2022).
Borja, Lauren J, and MV Ramana, 'Command and Control of India's Nuclear Arsenal' (2020) 3 *Journal for Peace and Nuclear Disarmament* 1.

Born, Hans, 'National Governance of Nuclear Weapons: Opportunities and Constraints' (*Geneva Centre for the Democratic Control of Armed Forces (DCAF), Policy Paper*, No 15, 2007), www.dcaf.ch/sites/default/files/publications/documents/PP15_Born.pdf.

Boulanin, Vincent, Lora Saalman, Petr Topychkanov, Fei Su, and Moa Peldán Carlsson, 'Artificial Intelligence, Strategic Stability and Nuclear Risk' (*SIPRI*, 2020), www.sipri.org/publications/2020/policy-reports/artificial-intelligence-strategic-stability-and-nuclear-risk.

Bradley, Curtis A, Jack L Goldsmith, and Oona A Hathaway, 'The Rise of Nonbinding International Agreements: An Empirical, Comparative, and Normative Analysis' (2023) 90 *University of Chicago Law Review* 1281.

Brandis, George, 'The Right of Self-Defence Against Imminent Armed Attack in International Law' (2018) 35 *Australian Year Book of International Law* 55.

Brixey-Williams, Sebastian, and Paul Ingram, 'Responsible Nuclear Sovereignty and the Future of the Global Nuclear Order' (*BASIC and the University of Birmingham's Institute for Conflict, Cooperation and Security*, 2017), https://basicint.org/wp-content/uploads/2018/06/Brixey-Williams-and-Ingram-Responsible-Nuclear-Sovereignty-Report-PDF_FINAL-2017.pdf.

Bruun, Laura, and Marta Bo, '"Constant Care" Must Be Taken to Address Bias in Military AI', *Humanitarian Law & Policy* (28 August 2025), https://blogs.icrc.org/law-and-policy/2025/08/28/constant-care-must-be-taken-to-address-bias-in-military-ai/.

Buchan, Russell, and Nicholas Tsagourias, *Regulating the Use of Force in International Law: Stability and Change* (Edward Elgar, 2021).

Buckland, Benjamin S, and Anna Marie Burdzy, *Progress and Opportunities: Challenges and Recommendations for Montreux Document Participants* (2nd ed, Geneva Centre for the Democratic Control of Armed Forces, 2015), www.montreuxdocument.org/pdf/Progress-and-Opportunities-Challenges-and-Recommendations-for-Montreux-Document-Participants-2nd-edition.pdf.

Byron, Christine, *War Crimes and Crimes Against Humanity in the Rome Statute of the International Criminal Court* (Manchester University Press, 2009).

Canada, *Joint Doctrine Manual: Law of Armed Conflict at the Operational and Tactical Levels* (B-GJ-005–104/FP-021, 2001).

Canada, *Parliamentary Debates* (Hansard), House of Commons, 6 May 2009, vol 144, no 052.

Canada, *Parliamentary Debates* (Hansard), House of Commons, 7 February 2011, vol 145, no 125.

Canada, *Parliamentary Debates* (Hansard), House of Commons, 9 February 2011, vol 145, no 127.

Casey-Maslen, Stuart, and Steven Haines, 'Defining an Armed Conflict', in *Hague Law Interpreted* (Bloomsbury Publishing, 2018).

Cassese, Antonio, 'The Martens Clause: Half a Loaf or Simply Pie in the Sky?' (2000) 11 *European Journal of International Law* 187.

Catalinac, Amy L, 'Why New Zealand Took Itself Out of ANZUS: Observing "Opposition for Autonomy" in Asymmetric Alliances' (2010) 6 *Foreign Policy Analysis* 317.

Ceccarelli, Michael, Rachael Harris, Bader Mahmoud, Diego Perez, and Shyla Sharma, 'Impact of Cyberattacks on Functionality of NC3 Systems and Strategic Deterrence' (*Carnegie Mellon University*) https://kilthub.cmu.edu/articles/report/Impact_of_Cyberattacks_on_Functionality_of_NC3_Systems_and_Strategic_Deterrence/21964826.

Chachko, Elena, and Ashley Deeks, 'Which States Support the "Unwilling and Unable" Test?', *Lawfare* (10 October 2016), www.lawfareblog.com/which-states-support-unwilling-and-unable-test.

Cheon, Myeongguk, 'DPRK'S NC3 System' (*NAPSNet Special Reports*, 6 June 2019), https://nautilus.org/napsnet/napsnet-special-reports/dprks-nc3-system/.

Cheong, Wook-Sik, 'The DPRK's Changed Nuclear Doctrine: Factors and Implications' (2023) 6 *Journal for Peace and Nuclear Disarmament* 136.

China, *Implementation of the Treaty on the Non-Proliferation of Nuclear Weapons in the People's Republic of China: Report Submitted by China*, 2020 Review Conference of the Parties to the Treaty on the Non-Proliferation of Nuclear Weapons, UN Doc NPT/CONF.2020/41 (16 November 2021).

China, *Implementation of the Treaty on the Non-Proliferation of Nuclear Weapons in the People's Republic of China: Report Submitted by China*, Preparatory Committee for the 2020 Review Conference of the Parties to the Treaty on the Non-Proliferation of Nuclear Weapons, UN Doc NPT/CONF.2020/PC.III/8 (29 April 2019).

Choi, Soo-Hyang, and Hyonhee Shin, 'North Korea Amends Constitution on Nuclear Policy, Cites US Provocations', *Reuters* (28 September 2023), www.reuters.com/world/asia-pacific/north-korea-parliament-amends-constitution-enshrine-nuclear-policy-kcna-2023-09-27/.

Cockayne, James, 'Regulating Private Military and Security Companies: The Content, Negotiation, Weaknesses and Promise of the Montreux Document' (2008) 13 *Journal of Conflict and Security Law* 401.

Cohen, Avner, 'Israel's NC3 Profile: Opaque Nuclear Governance' (*NAPSNet Special Reports*, 11 October 2019), https://nautilus.org/napsnet/napsnet-special-reports/israels-nc3-profile-opaque-nuclear-governance/.

Cohen, Avner, *The Worst-Kept Secret: Israel's Bargain with the Bomb* (Columbia University Press, 2010).

Congressional Research Service (United States), 'The Department of Defense's Use of Private Security Contractors in Afghanistan and Iraq: Background, Analysis, and Options for Congress' (*CRS Report*, No R40835, updated 13 May 2011).

Corten, Olivier, 'The "Unwilling or Unable" Test: Has It Been, and Could It Be, Accepted?' (2016) 29 *Leiden Journal of International Law* 777.

Council of the European Union, 'Annual Progress Report on the Implementation of the European Union Strategy Against the Proliferation of Weapons of Mass Destruction (2019), 2020/C 341/01', *Official Journal of the European Union*, 22020/C 341/01 (13 October 2020).

Crawford, Emily, *Identifying the Enemy: Civilian Participation in Armed Conflict* (Oxford University Press, 2015).

Crawford, Emily, *Non-Binding Norms in International Humanitarian Law: Efficacy, Legitimacy, and Legality* (Oxford University Press, 2021).

Crawford, James, *State Responsibility: The General Part* (Cambridge University Press, 2013).

Cryer, Robert, Håkan Friman, Darryl Robinson, and Elizabeth Wilmshurst, *An Introduction to International Criminal Law and Procedure* (3rd ed, Cambridge University Press, 2014).

Cullen, Anthony, *The Concept of Non-International Armed Conflict in International Humanitarian Law* (Cambridge University Press, 2010).

Cunningham, Fiona S, 'Nuclear Command, Control, and Communications Systems of the People's Republic of China' (*NAPSNet Special Reports*, 18 July 2019), https://nautilus.org/napsnet/napsnet-special-reports/nuclear-command-control-and-communications-systems-of-the-peoples-republic-of-china/.

Dalton, Toby, 'Much Ado About India's No-First-Use Nuke Policy' (*Carnegie Endowment for International Peace*, 26 September 2019) (originally published in *India Global Business*, September 2019), https://carnegieendowment.org/2019/09/26/much-ado-about-india-s-no-first-use-nuke-policy-pub-79952.

Danish Ministry of Defence, *Military Manual on International Law Relevant to Danish Armed Forces in International Operations* (updated 12 October 2020).

Democratic Control of Armed Forces, 'What Is DCAF?', www.dcaf.ch/about-us.

Doswald-Beck, Louise (ed), *San Remo Manual on International Law Applicable to Armed Conflicts at Sea* (Cambridge University Press, 1995).

Doswald-Beck, Louise, 'The San Remo Manual on International Law Applicable to Armed Conflicts at Sea' (1995) 89 *American Journal of International Law* 192.

Eichensehr, Kristen, 'Review of *Tallinn Manual on the International Law Applicable to Cyber Warfare*' (2014) 108 *American Journal of International Law* 588.

Ellis, Jaye, 'Shades of Grey: Soft Law and the Validity of Public International Law' (2012) 25 *Leiden Journal of International Law* 313.

Elsea, Jennifer K, 'Private Security Contractors in Iraq and Afghanistan: Legal Issues' (*CRS Report*, No R40991, 7 January 2010).

Emanuelli, Claude C, 'Comments on the ICRC Study on Customary International Humanitarian Law' (2007) 44 *Canadian Yearbook of International Law* 437.

Erästö, Tytti, 'The Role of Umbrella States in the Global Nuclear Order' (*SIPRI Insights on Peace and Security*, No 2023/06, June 2023), www.sipri.org/publications/2023/sipri-insights-peace-and-security/role-umbrella-states-global-nuclear-order.

European Commission for Democracy through Law (Venice Commission), *2009 Annual Activity Report* (Council of Europe, 2010).

European Commission for Democracy through Law (Venice Commission), 'Report on Private Military and Security Firms and Erosion of the State Monopoly on the Use of Force' (*Study*, No 531/2009, 29 June 2009).

European Parliament, 'Joint Answer Given by High Representative/Vice-President Ashton on Behalf of the Commission', 2 August 2012, *Official Journal of the European Union*, vol 56, C 262E/132 (11 September 2013).

European Parliament, *Resolution of 8 October 2013 on Corruption in the Public and Private Sectors: The Impact on Human Rights in Third Countries* (2013/2074(INI)), P7_TA(2013)0394.

European Parliament, *Resolution of 21 January 2016 on Estonian and UK Seamen under Detention in India* (2016/2522(RSP)), P8_TA(2016)0022.

European Parliament, *Resolution of 25 November 2021 on the Human Rights Violations by Private Military and Security Companies, Particularly the Wagner Group* (2021/2982(RSP)).

European Parliament, Committee of Foreign Affairs, *Draft Report on Human Rights Concerns in Private Military and Security Companies' Operations Affecting Third Countries* (2018/2154(INI), 17 July 2018).

Farabaugh, Bryce, and sdaniels, 'Bad Idea: Integrating Artificial Intelligence with Nuclear Command, Control, and Communications', *Defense360* (3 December 2019), https://defense360.csis.org/bad-idea-integrating-artificial-intelligence-with-nuclear-command-control-and-communications/.

Federal Council (Switzerland), 'International Code of Conduct for Private Security Service Providers – Consensus on Oversight Mechanism' (22 February 2013), www.admin.ch/gov/en/start/dokumentation/medien-mitteilungen.msg-id-47889.html.

Fellmeth, Aaron X, and Maurice Horwitz, *Guide to Latin in International Law* (Oxford University Press, 2009).

Fleck, Dieter, 'Searching for International Rules Applicable to Cyber Warfare – A Critical First Assessment of the New *Tallinn Manual*' (2013) 18 *Journal of Conflict and Security Law* 331.

Francioni, Francesco, 'International "Soft Law": A Contemporary Assessment', in Vaughan Lowe and Malgosia Fitzmaurice (eds), *Fifty Years of the International Court of Justice: Essays in Honour of Sir Robert Jennings* (Cambridge University Press, 1996).

Franck, Thomas M, *The Power of Legitimacy Among Nations* (Oxford University Press, 1990).

Franck, Thomas M, 'The Power of Legitimacy and the Legitimacy of Power: International Law in an Age of Power Disequilibrium' (2006) 100 *American Journal of International Law* 88.

French Ministère de la Défense, 'Manuel de droit des conflits armés' (2012), https://defenseetsecuriteinternationale.files.wordpress.com/2013/10/manuel_de_droit_des_conflits_armes.pdf.

French Ministère des Armées, 'Manuel de droit des opérations militaires' (2022), www.defense.gouv.fr/sites/default/files/sga/Manuel%20de%20droit%20des%20op%C3%A9rations%20militaires_%C3%A9dition%202022.pdf.

Future of Life Institute, 'Risks of Artificial Intelligence in Nuclear Command, Control and Communications (NC3): Primer & Policy Options for Risk Mitigation' (July 2023), https://futureoflife.org/fli_ai_nc3_policy_primer/.

Geneva Academy, 'The International Code of Conduct for Private Security Service Providers' (*Academy Briefing*, No 4, August 2013).

Geneva Centre for the Democratic Control of Armed Forces, *The Montreux Document: A Mapping Study on Outreach and Implementation* (DCAF, 2017).

Genève Internationale, 'Geneva Academy of International Humanitarian Law and Human Rights', www.geneve-int.ch/Geneva-Academy.

German Bundestag, 'Germany's Global Role in Nuclear Disarmament and Non-Proliferation' (WD 2–3000 – 044/18, 11 April 2018), www.bundestag.de/resource/blob/557668/d9de6462b82653652b18fbb914834e82/WD-2-044-18-pdf-data.pdf.

Gogna, Sanjana, 'The Nasr and India's Nuclear Command Structure, Strategy and Doctrine' (2023) 42 *Comparative Strategy* 50.

Gower, John, 'United Kingdom: Nuclear Weapon Command, Control, and Communications: Technology for Global Security Special Report' (*Tech4GS Special Reports*, 15 August 2019), https://securityandtechnology.org/wp-content/uploads/2020/07/gower_uk_nc3_report_IST.pdf.

Gray, Christine, *International Law and the Use of Force* (4th ed, Oxford University Press, 2018).

Gronlund, Lisbeth, David Wright, and Steve Fetter, 'An Expert Proposal: How to Limit Presidential Authority to Order the Use of Nuclear Weapons', *Bulletin of the Atomic Scientists* (8 January 2021), https://thebulletin.org/2021/01/an-expert-proposal-how-to-limit-presidential-authority-to-order-the-use-of-nuclear-weapons/.

Guzman, Andrew T, and Timothy Meyer, 'Soft Law', in Eugene Kontorovich and Francesco Parisi (eds), *Economic Analysis of International Law* (Edward Elgar, 2015).

Hague Code of Conduct Executive Secretariat, 'Frequently Asked Questions about HCoC' (March 2024), www.hcoc.at/what-is-hcoc/frequently-asked-questions.html.

Hague Code of Conduct Executive Secretariat, 'The Hague Code of Conduct Against Ballistic Missile Proliferation (HCoC)' (March 2024), www.hcoc.at/.

Hague Code of Conduct Executive Secretariat, 'List of HCoC Subscribing States' (January 2024), www.hcoc.at/subscribing-states/list-of-hcoc-subscribing-states.html.

Haque, Adil Ahmad, 'Necessity and Proportionality in International Law', in Larry May (ed), *The Cambridge Handbook of the Just War* (Cambridge University Press, 2018).

Harvey, John R, 'U.S. Nuclear Command and Control for the 21st Century' (*NAPSNet Special Reports*, 24 May 2019), https://nautilus.org/napsnet/napsnet-special-reports/u-s-nuclear-command-and-control-for-the-21st-century/.

Hayes, Peter, 'Nuclear Command-and-Control in the Quantum Era' (*NAPSNet Blue Peter*, 29 March 2018), https://nautilus.org/napsnet/nuclear-command-and-control-in-the-quantum-era/.

Hayes, Peter, 'Nuclear Command, Control, and Communications (NC3) in Asia-Pacific' (*NAPSNet Special Reports*, 22 September 2021), https://nautilus.org/napsnet/napsnet-special-reports/nuclear-command-control-and-communications-nc3-in-asia-pacific/.

Hayes, Peter, Binoy Kampmark, Philip Reiner, and Deborah Gordon, 'Synthesis Report, NC3 Systems and Strategic Stability: A Global Overview' (*Tech4GS Special Reports*, 6 May 2019), https://securityandtechnology.org/wp-content/uploads/2024/10/nc3_synthesis_report_may_6_2019_IST.pdf.

Heintschel von Heinegg, Wolff, 'The Law of Armed Conflict at Sea', in Dieter Fleck (ed), *The Handbook of International Humanitarian Law* (3rd ed, Oxford University Press, 2013).

Heintschel von Heinegg, Wolff, 'Maritime Warfare', in Andrew Clapham and Paola Gaeta (eds), *The Oxford Handbook of International Law in Armed Conflict* (Oxford University Press, 2014).

Henckaerts, Jean-Marie, and Louise Doswald-Beck (eds), *Customary International Humanitarian Law* (Cambridge University Press, 2005).

Hruby, Jill, and M Nina Miller, 'Assessing and Managing the Benefits and Risks of Artificial Intelligence in Nuclear-Weapon Systems' (*Nuclear Threat Initiative*, 2021), www.nti.org/analysis/articles/assessing-and-managing-the-benefits-and-risks-of-artificial-intelligence-in-nuclear-weapon-systems/.

Hughes, David, and Yahli Shereshevsky, 'State-Academic Lawmaking' (2023) 64 *Harvard International Law Journal* 253.

Hurd, Ian, 'Legitimacy and Authority in International Politics' (1999) 53 *International Organisation* 379.

Hwang, Ildo, 'North Korea's Nuclear Command and Control Estimate: Variables and Trends' (2021) 33 *Korean Journal of Defense Analysis* 617.

ICAN, 'Australia's Reassessment of the Treaty on the Prohibition of Nuclear Weapons' (15 November 2022), www.icanw.org/australia_tpnw.

Independent International Fact-Finding Mission on the Conflict in Georgia, 'Report' (2009), www.mpil.de/en/pub/publications/archive/independent_international_fact.cfm.

Indian Ministry of External Affairs, 'India's View on the Treaty on the Prohibition of Nuclear Weapons' (*Press Release*, 22 January 2021), www.mea.gov.in/press-releases.htm?dtl/33409/Indias+view+on+the+Treaty+on+the+Prohibition+of+Nuclear+Weapons.

Indurthy, Rathnam, *India–Pakistan Wars and the Kashmir Crisis* (Routledge, 2019).

Information Memorandum from the President's Special Assistant (Rostow) to President Johnson, 12 December 1968, reprinted in *Foreign Relations of the United States, 1964–1968, Volume XX: Arab-Israeli Dispute, 1967–68*, https://history.state.gov/historicaldocuments/frus1964-68v20/d349.

International Code of Conduct Association, *Annual Report 2013–2014* (ICoCA, 2014).

International Code of Conduct Association, 'Members', https://icoca.ch/membership/.

International Commission of Inquiry on Darfur, 'Report to the United Nations Secretary-General Pursuant to Security Council Resolution 1564 of 18 September 2004' (25 January 2005), www2.ohchr.org/english/darfur.htm.

International Committee of the Red Cross, 'Air and Naval Warfare', www.icrc.org/en/law-and-policy/air-and-naval-warfare.

International Committee of the Red Cross, *Commentary on the Second Geneva Convention: Convention (II) for the Amelioration of the Condition of the Wounded, Sick and Shipwrecked Members of Armed Forces at Sea* (2nd ed, 2017), https://ihl-databases.icrc.org/en/ihl-treaties/gcii-1949?activeTab=1949GCs-APs-and-commentaries.

International Committee of the Red Cross, Customary IHL Database, Introduction, https://ihl-databases.icrc.org/en/customary-ihl/v1/in.

International Committee of the Red Cross, Customary IHL Database, Nuclear Weapons, https://ihl-databases.icrc.org/en/customary-ihl/v1/nuwe.

International Committee of the Red Cross, Customary IHL Database, Rule 6: Civilians' Loss of Protection from Attack, https://ihl-databases.icrc.org/en/customary-ihl/v1/rule6.

International Committee of the Red Cross, Customary IHL Database, Rule 72: Poison, https://ihl-databases.icrc.org/en/customary-ihl/v1/rule72.

International Committee of the Red Cross, Customary IHL Database, Rule 145: Reprisals, https://ihl-databases.icrc.org/en/customary-ihl/v1/rule145.

International Committee of the Red Cross, Customary IHL Database, Rules 43–45, https://ihl-databases.icrc.org/en/customary-ihl/v1.

International Committee of the Red Cross, *Resolution 1: International Humanitarian Law: From Law to Action, Report on the Follow-up to the International Conference for the Protection of War Victims*, 26th International Conference of the Red Cross and Red Crescent, Geneva, 3–7 December 1995, reprinted in (1996) 310 *International Review of the Red Cross* 58.

International Committee of the Red Cross, *Resolution VII: Work on International Humanitarian Law in Armed Conflicts at Sea and on Land*, adopted at the final plenary meeting on 31 October 1986, 25th International Conference of the Red Cross, Geneva, 23–31 October 1986, reprinted in (1986) 26 *International Review of the Red Cross* 340.

International Criminal Court, *Situation on Registered Vessels of Comoros, Greece and Cambodia: Article 53(1) Report* (6 November 2014).

International Law Commission, 'Analytical Guide to the Work of the International Law Commission: Crimes Against Humanity', https://legal.un.org/ilc/guide/7_7.shtml.

International Law Commission, *Report of the International Law Commission on the Work of Its Fifty-third Session (23 April–1 June and 2 July–10 August 2001)*, UN Doc A/56/10 (2001).

International Law Commission, *Report of the International Law Commission on the Work of Its Sixty-third Session (26 April–3 June and 4 July–12 August 2011)*, UN Doc A/66/10 (2011).

International Law Commission, *Report of the International Law Commission on the Work of Its Sixty-eighth Session (2 May–10 June and 4 July–12 August 2016)*, Supplement No 10, UN Doc A/71/10 (2024).

International Law Commission, *Report of the International Law Commission on the Work of Its Seventy-first Session (29 April–7 June and 8 July–9 August 2019)*, UN Doc A/74/10 (2019).

International Law Commission, *Report of the International Law Commission on the Work of Its Seventy-third Session (18 April–3 June and 4 July–5 August 2022)*, UN Doc A/77/10 (2022).

International Law Commission, *Second Report on Protection of the Environment in Relation to Armed Conflicts by Marja Lehto, Special Rapporteur*, Seventy-first Session, 29 April–7 June 2019 and 8 July–9 August 2019, UN Doc A/CN.4/728 (27 March 2019).

International Law Commission, *Second Report on the Protection of the Environment in Relation to Armed Conflicts, Submitted by Marie G Jacobsson,*

Special Rapporteur, Sixty-seventh Session, 4 May–5 June and 6 July–7 August 2015, UN Doc A/CN.4/685 (28 May 2015).

International Law Commission, *Summary Record of the 3275th Meeting*, UN Doc A/CN.4/SR.3275 (22 September 2015).

International Maritime Organization, Maritime Safety Committee, *Piracy and Armed Robbery Against Ships: Development of Guidance for the Industry on the Employment of Private Armed Security Service Providers to Deter and Counter Piracy Against Ships, Submitted by the Philippines, Singapore, BIMCO and ICS*, MSC/89/18/5 (8 March 2011).

Israeli, Ofer, 'Israel's Nuclear Amimut Policy and Its Consequences' (2015) 21 *Israel Affairs* 541.

Ivanenko, Vitaliy, 'The Origins, Causes and Enduring Significance of the Martens Clause: A View from Russia' (2022) 104 *International Review of the Red Cross* 1708.

Janssens, Pauline Charlotte, and Jan Wouters, 'Informal International Law-Making: A Way Around the Deadlock of International Humanitarian Law?' (2022) 104 *International Review of the Red Cross* 2111.

Jonas, David S, and Bryn McWhorter, 'Nuclear Launch Authority: Too Big a Decision for Just the President' (*Arms Control Association*, June 2021), www.armscontrol.org/act/2021-06/features/nuclear-launch-authority-too-big-decision-just-president.

Kallenborn, Zachary, 'Giving an AI Control of Nuclear Weapons: What Could Possibly Go Wrong?', *Bulletin of the Atomic Scientists* (1 February 2022), https://thebulletin.org/2022/02/giving-an-ai-control-of-nuclear-weapons-what-could-possibly-go-wrong/.

Kasapoğlu, Can, 'Turkey and Nuclear Command, Control and Communications' (*Tech4GS Special Reports*, 27 June 2019), https://securityandtechnology.org/wp-content/uploads/2024/10/kasapoglu_turkey_nc3_IST-1.pdf.

Kassoti, Eva, 'Beyond State Consent? International Legal Scholarship and the Challenge of Informal International Law-Making' (2016) 63 *Netherlands International Law Review* 99.

Kawaguchi, Yoriko, 'Speech by Minister for Foreign Affairs Yoriko Kawaguchi to the Conference on Disarmament' (4 September 2003), www.disarm.emb-japan.go.jp/Statements/030904CD.htm.

KCNA Watch, 'Law on DPRK's Policy on Nuclear Forces Promulgated', *Korean Central News Agency* (9 September 2022), https://kcnawatch.org/newstream/1662687258-950776986/law-on-dprks-policy-on-nuclear-forces-promulgated/.

Keller, Helen, 'Codes of Conduct and Their Implementation: The Question of Legitimacy', in Rüdiger Wolfrum and Volker Röben (eds), *Legitimacy in International Law* (Springer, 2008).

Kelly, Andrew, *ANZUS and the Early Cold War: Strategy and Diplomacy Between Australia, New Zealand and the United States, 1945–1956* (Open Book, 2018).

Kessing, Peter Vedel, 'The Use of Soft Law in Regulating Armed Conflict: From *Jus in Bello* to "Soft Law *in Bello*"?', in Stéphanie Lagoutte, Thomas Gammeltoft-Hansen, and John Cerrone (eds), *Tracing the Roles of Soft Law in Human Rights* (Oxford University Press, 2016).

Khan, Feroz Hassan, 'Nuclear Command, Control and Communications (NC3): The Case of Pakistan' (*NAPSNet Special Reports*, 26 September 2019), https://nautilus.org/napsnet/napsnet-special-reports/nuclear-command-control-and-communications-nc3-the-case-of-pakistan/.

Kidwai, Khalid, '25 Years of Yom Takbeer: Promoting Peace, Stability and Development' (*Speech*, Arms Control and Disarmament Centre/Institute of Strategic Studies Islamabad, 24 May 2023), https://issi.org.pk/speech-by-lt-gen-retd-khalid-kidwai-advisor-national-command-authority-and-former-dg-spd-on-25th-youme-e-takbeer/.

Kleffner, Jann, 'Section IX of the ICRC Interpretive Guidance on Direct Participation in Hostilities: The End of *Jus in Bello* Proportionality as We Know It?' (2012) 45 *Israel Law Review* 35.

Klingner, Bruce, 'The Troubling New Changes to North Korea's Nuclear Doctrine' (*Backgrounder* [The Heritage Foundation], No 3729, 17 October 2022), www.heritage.org/asia/report/the-troubling-new-changes-north-koreas-nuclear-doctrine.

Kodner, Lior, 'Podcast Interview with Ehud Barak', *Haaretz* (26 March 2019), www.haaretz.co.il/digital/podcast/.premium-1.7059848.

Kravik, Andreas Motzfeldt, 'An Analysis of Stagnation in Multilateral Law-Making – and Why the Law of the Sea Has Transcended the Stagnation Trend' (2021) 34 *Leiden Journal of International Law* 935.

Kristensen, Hans M, and Matt Korda, 'Estimating World Nuclear Forces: An Overview and Assessment of Sources' (*SIPRI*, 14 June 2021), www.sipri.org/commentary/topical-backgrounder/2021/estimating-world-nuclear-forces-overview-and-assessment-sources.

Kristensen, Hans M, and Matt Korda, 'Israeli Nuclear Weapons 2021' (2022) 78 *Bulletin of the Atomic Scientists* 38.

Kristensen, Hans M, and Matt Korda, 'World Nuclear Forces', in Stockholm International Peace Research Institute (ed), *SIPRI Yearbook 2025: Armaments, Disarmament and International Security* (2025), www.sipri.org/sites/default/files/SIPRIYB25c06%266A.pdf.

Kristensen, Hans M, Matt Korda, Eliana Johns, and Mackenzie Knight, 'The Changing Nuclear Landscape in Europe' (2025) 81 *Bulletin of the Atomic Scientists* 485.

Kristensen, Hans M, Matt Korda, Eliana Johns, and Mackenzie Knight, 'Chinese Nuclear Weapons, 2025' (2025) 81 *Bulletin of the Atomic Scientists* 135.

Kristensen, Hans M, Matt Korda, Eliana Johns, and Mackenzie Knight, 'French Nuclear Weapons, 2025' (2025) 81 *Bulletin of the Atomic Scientists* 313.

Kristensen, Hans M, Matt Korda, Eliana Johns, and Mackenzie Knight, 'Indian Nuclear Weapons, 2024' (2024) 80 *Bulletin of the Atomic Scientists* 326.

Kristensen, Hans M, Matt Korda, Eliana Johns, and Mackenzie Knight, 'North Korean Nuclear Weapons, 2024' (2024) 80 *Bulletin of the Atomic Scientists* 251.

Kristensen, Hans M, Matt Korda, Eliana Johns, and Mackenzie Knight, 'Pakistan Nuclear Weapons, 2025' (2025) 81 *Bulletin of the Atomic Scientists* 386.

Kristensen, Hans M, Matt Korda, Eliana Johns, and Mackenzie Knight, 'Russian Nuclear Weapons, 2025' (2025) 81 *Bulletin of the Atomic Scientists* 208.

Kristensen, Hans M, Matt Korda, Eliana Johns, and Mackenzie Knight, 'United Kingdom Nuclear Weapons, 2024' (2024) 80 *Bulletin of the Atomic Scientists* 394.

Kristensen, Hans M, Matt Korda, Eliana Johns, and Mackenzie Knight, 'United States Nuclear Weapons, 2025' (2025) 81 *Bulletin of the Atomic Scientists* 53.

Kwon, Edward, 'North Korea's Nuclear Strategy and the Direction of WMD Development' (2020) 33 *Journal of East Asian Affairs* 276.

Levite, Ariel E, Lyu Jinghua, George Perkovich, Lu Chuanying, Xu Manshu, Li Bin, and Yang Fan, 'China-U.S. Cyber-Nuclear C3 Stability' (*Carnegie Endowment for International Peace*, April 2021), https://carnegieendowment.org/research/2021/04/china-us-cyber-nuclear-c3-stability.

Lewis, Jeffrey G, and Scott D Sagan, 'The Nuclear Necessity Principle: Making U.S. Targeting Policy Conform with Ethics & the Laws of War' (2016) 145 *Dædalus: Journal of the American Academy of Arts & Sciences* 62.

Lewis, Jeffrey G, and Bruno Tertrais, 'The Finger on the Button: The Authority to Use Nuclear Weapons in Nuclear-Armed States' (*Occasional Paper 45*, James Martin Center for Nonproliferation Studies, February 2019), https://nonproliferation.org/wp-content/uploads/2019/02/Finger-on-the-Nuclear-Button.pdf.

Lindsay, Jon, 'Cyber Operations and Nuclear Weapons' (*Tech4GS Special Reports*, 20 June 2019), https://securityandtechnology.org/wp-content/uploads/2020/07/lindsay_cyber-nc3_IST-1.pdf.

MacDonald, Eryn, 'Whose Finger Is on the Button? Nuclear Launch Authority in the United States and Other Nations' (*Issue Brief*, Union of Concerned Scientists, 2017), www.ucsusa.org/sites/default/files/attach/2017/11/Launch-Authority.pdf.

Mayntz, Renate, 'Legitimacy and Compliance in Transnational Governance' (*MPIfG Working Paper*, No 10/5, Max Planck Institute for the Study of Societies, 2010).

McIntyre, W David, *Background to the Anzus Pact: Policy-Making, Strategy and Diplomacy, 1945–55* (Palgrave Macmillan, 1995).

Mills, Claire, 'Nuclear Weapons at a Glance: India and Pakistan' (*Research Briefing*, House of Commons Library, 29 July 2022), https://researchbriefings.files.parliament.uk/documents/CBP-9070/CBP-9070.pdf.

Mills, Claire, 'Nuclear Weapons Profile: Israel' (*Research Briefing*, House of Commons Library, 29 July 2022), https://researchbriefings.files.parliament.uk/documents/CBP-9075/CBP-9075.pdf.

Ministry of Foreign Affairs, Japan, 'Diplomatic Bluebook 2023: Japanese Diplomacy and International Situation in 2022' (2023), www.ec.emb-japan.go.jp/files/100406514.pdf.

Ministry of Foreign Affairs of the Russian Federation, 'Fundamentals of State Policy of the Russian Federation on Nuclear Deterrence' (19 November 2024), www.mid.ru/en/foreign_policy/international_safety/1434131/.

Miraglia, Sébastien, 'Deadly or Impotent? Nuclear Command and Control in Pakistan' (2013) 36 *Journal of Strategic Studies* 841.

Missile Technology Control Regime, *Equipment, Software and Technology Annex*, MTCR/TEM/2024/Annex (14 March 2024), www.mtcr.info/en/mtcr-annex.

Missile Technology Control Regime, 'Frequently Asked Questions: 4. What Is the Purpose of the MTCR?', www.mtcr.info/en/faq.

Moir, Lindsay, *Reappraising the Resort to Force: International Law, Jus ad Bellum and the War on Terror* (Hart, 2010).

Montreux Document Forum, 'Historical Timeline', www.mdforum.ch/en/history.

National Institute of Standards and Technology, 'jamming', Computer Security and Resource Centre, https://csrc.nist.gov/glossary/term/jamming.

National Institute of Standards and Technology, 'spoofing', Computer Security and Resource Centre, https://csrc.nist.gov/glossary/term/spoofing.

NATO, *NATO 2022 Strategic Concept*, adopted by Heads of State and Government at the NATO Summit in Madrid (29 June 2022) www.nato.int/cps/en/natohq/topics_210907.htm.

NATO, *NATO Standard AJP–3.23: Allied Joint Doctrine for Countering Weapons of Mass Destruction in Military Operations* (NATO, September 2023).

NATO, 'Official Texts', https://natolibguides.info/missiledefence/documents.

Nautilus Institute, Stanley Center for Peace and Security, and Technology for Global Security, *Last Chance: Communicating at the Nuclear Brink Scenarios and Solutions Workshop Synthesis Report* (14 May 2020).

New Zealand Foreign Affairs & Trade, 'The Nuclear Non-Proliferation Treaty (NPT)', www.mfat.govt.nz/en/peace-rights-and-security/disarmament/weapons-of-mass-destruction#bookmark0.

Non-Aligned Movement, *Ministerial Meeting of the Coordinating Bureau of the Non-Aligned Movement (CoB-NAM): Final Document*, NAM 2019/CoB/Doc.1 (2019).

Norway, *Manual i krigens folkerett* [Manual on the International Law of War] (Forsvarets høgskole, 2013).

Norway, Ministry of Trade and Fisheries, 'Meld. St. 10 (2019–2020): Høytflyvende satellitter – jordnære formal, En strategi for norsk romvirksomhet' [Report to the Storting (2019–2020): High-flying Satellites – Earth-based Purposes. A Strategy for Norwegian Space Activities] (2019), www.regjeringen.no/no/dokumenter/meld.-st.-10-20192020/id2682361/?ch=8.

Norway, Permanent Mission to the United Nations in New York, 'Statement by Permanent Representative Ambassador Merete Fjeld Brattested in the General Debate of the First Committee' (3 October 2023), www.norway.no/en/missions/un/statements/general-assembly-plenary/2023/statement-in-the-general-debate/1c-opening-statement/.

Nuclear Threat Initiative, 'Nuclear Disarmament Israel' (*Fact Sheet*, 15 November 2023), www.nti.org/analysis/articles/israel-nuclear-disarmament/.

O'Connell, Mary Ellen, 'Defining Armed Conflict' (2008) 13 *Journal of Conflict and Security Law* 393.

O'Meara, Chris, *Necessity and Proportionality and the Right of Self-Defence in International Law* (Oxford University Press, 2021).

Office of the Deputy Assistant Secretary of Defense for Nuclear Matters, *Nuclear Matters Handbook 2020 [Revised]* (2020), www.acq.osd.mil/ncbdp/nm//NMHB2020rev/.

Official Records of the Assembly of States Parties to the Rome Statute of the International Criminal Court, First Session, New York, 3–10 September 2002 (United Nations, Sales No E.03.V.2 and corrigendum).

Official Records of the Review Conference of the Rome Statute of the International Criminal Court, Kampala, 31 May – 11 June 2010 (International Criminal Court, RC/11, 2010).

Palmer, Geoffrey, Alvaro Uribe, Joseph Ciechanover Itzhar, and Süleyman Özdem Sanberk, *Report of the Secretary-General's Panel of Inquiry on the 31 May 2010 Flotilla Incident* (July 2011).

Pandit, Rajat, 'Narendra Modi Has His Finger Now on India's Nuclear Button', *Times of India* (27 May 2014), http://timesofindia.indiatimes.com/news/Narendra-Modi-has-his-finger-now-on-Indias-nuclearbutton/articleshow/35625045.cms.

Pant, Harsh V, 'India's Nuclear Doctrine and Command Structure: Implications for India and the World' (2005) 24 *Comparative Strategy* 277.

Parks, W Hays, 'Part IX of the ICRC "Direct Participation in Hostilities" Study: No Mandate, No Expertise, and Legally Incorrect' (2010) 42 *New York University Journal of International Law and Politics* 769.

Pauwelyn, Joost, 'Informal International Lawmaking: Framing the Concept and Research Questions', in Joost Pauwelyn, Ramses Wessel, and Jan Wouters (eds), *Informal International Lawmaking* (Oxford University Press, 2012).

Pauwelyn, Joost, Ramses Wessel, and Jan Wouters (eds), *Informal International Lawmaking* (Oxford University Press, 2012).

Pelopidas, Benoît, 'France: Nuclear Command, Control, and Communications' (*NAPSNet Special Reports*, 10 June 2019), https://nautilus.org/napsnet/napsnet-special-reports/france-nuclear-command-control-and-communications/.

Permanent Council of the Organization of American States, Committee on Juridical and Political Affairs, *Final Report: Special Meeting on International Humanitarian Law [AG/RES. 2507 (XXXIX-O/09)]* (29 January 2010).

Permanent Mission of the Federated States of Micronesia to the United Nations, *Statement by the Micronesian Delegation*, 76th Session of the United Nations General Assembly, Agenda Item 124: Strengthening of the United Nations System (8 June 2022), https://unmission.fm/wp-content/uploads/2022/06/Micronesia-DPRK-item-124.pdf.

Permanent Mission of Switzerland to the United Nations, *Note Verbale Dated 7 June 2012 from the Permanent Mission of Switzerland to the United Nations Addressed to the Secretary-General of the United Nations*, 202/12 SXN/ULN (7 June 2012).

Peters, Anne, Heike Krieger, and Leonhard Kreuzer, 'Due Diligence in International Law: Dissecting the Leitmotif of Current Accountability Debates', in Heike Krieger, Anne Peters, and Leonhard Kreuzer (eds), *Due Diligence in the International Legal Order* (Oxford University Press, 2020).

Pictet, Jean (ed), *Commentary to the Third Geneva Convention Relative to the Treatment of Prisoners of War* (ICRC, 1960).

Program on Humanitarian Policy and Conflict Research at Harvard University, *Manual on International Law Applicable to Air and Missile Warfare* (HPCR, 2009).

Public Commission to Examine the Maritime Incident of 31 May 2010 (Turkel Commission), *Report, Part One* (January 2011).

Republic of Korea, '2010 Defence White Paper' (2011), www.files.ethz.ch/isn/155720/South%20Korea%202010_eng-1.pdf.

République Française, 'National Strategic Review 2022' (November 2022), www.sgdsn.gouv.fr/files/files/rns-uk-20221202.pdf.

Reuters, 'The Chain of Command for Potential Russian Nuclear Strikes', *Reuters* (3 March 2022), www.reuters.com/world/europe/what-is-chain-command-potential-russian-nuclear-strikes-2022-03-02/.

Risse, Thomas, 'Transnational Governance and Legitimacy', in Arthur Benz and Yannis Papadopoulos (eds), *Governance and Democracy: Comparing National, European and International Experiences* (Routledge, 2006).

Ronzitti, Natalino, 'Rescuing Nationals Abroad Revisited' (2019) 24 *Journal of Conflict and Security Law* 431.

Royal Navy, 'HMNB Clyde', www.royalnavy.mod.uk/our-organisation/bases-and-stations/naval-base/clyde.

Ryabikhin, Leonid, 'Russia's NC3 and Early Warning Systems' (*NAPSNet Special Reports*, 11 July 2019), https://nautilus.org/napsnet/napsnet-special-reports/russias-nc3-and-early-warning-systems/.

Sadat, Leila Nadya, *The International Criminal Court and the Transformation of International Law: Justice for the New Millenium* (Brill, 2002).

Sagan, Scott D, and Allen S Weiner, 'The Illegality of Targeting Civilians by Way of Belligerent Reprisal: Implications for U.S. Nuclear Doctrine', *Just Security* (10 May 2021), www.justsecurity.org/76049/the-illegality-of-targeting-civilians-by-way-of-belligerent-reprisal-implications-for-u-s-nuclear-doctrine/.

Sagan, Scott D, and Allen S Weiner, 'The Rule of Law and the Role of Strategy in U.S. Nuclear Doctrine' (2021) 45 *International Security* 126.

Sanders-Zakre, Alicia, and Kelsey Davenport, 'Is India Shifting Nuclear Doctrine?', *Arms Control Today* (May 2017), www.armscontrol.org/act/2017-05/news/india-shifting-nuclear-doctrine.

Schachter, Oscar, 'The Twilight Existence of Nonbinding International Agreements' (1977) 71 *American Journal of International Law* 296.

Schack, Marc, 'Resisting Clarity: Scandinavian Ambiguity in the "Unable or Unwilling"-Debate' (2021) 90 *Nordic Journal of International Law* 31.

Schmitt, Michael N (ed), *Tallinn Manual on the International Law Applicable to Cyber Warfare* (Cambridge University Press, 2013).

Shaheen, Salma, *Nuclear Command and Control Norms: A Comparative Study* (Routledge, 2018).

Shin, Hyonhee, and Ju-min Park, 'South Korea Holds Rare Air Raid Drill, But Many Citizens Ignore It', *Reuters* (23 August 2023), www.reuters.com/world/asia-pacific/south-korea-hold-first-nationwide-defence-drills-6-years-amid-north-threats-2023-08-23/.

Simma, Bruno, Daniel-Erasmus Khan, Georg Nolte, Andreas Paulus, and Nikolai Wessendorf (eds), *The Charter of the United Nations: A Commentary, Volume I* (3rd ed, Oxford University Press, 2012).

Singer, PW, and Ma Xiu, 'China's Ambiguous Missile Strategy Is Risky', *Popular Science* (11 May 2020), www.popsci.com/story/blog-network/eastern-arsenal/china-nuclear-conventional-missiles/.

Smith, Shane, 'Cyber Threats and Weapons of Mass Destruction', *CSWMD Proceedings* (National Defense University, June 2021), https://inss.ndu.edu/Portals/68/Documents/wmd-proceedings/CSWMD%20Proceedings%20Jun%2021%20PQ.pdf.

Smith, Shane, and Paul Berstein, 'North Korean Nuclear Command and Control: Alternatives and Implications' (*Strategic Trends Research Initiative*, Defence Threat Reduction Agency, August 2022), https://wmdcenter.ndu.edu/Portals/97/Documents/Publications/NK-Nuclear-Command-and-Control_Report.pdf.

Snyder, Francis, 'The Effectiveness of European Community Law: Institutions, Processes, Tools and Techniques' (1993) 56 *Modern Law Review* 19.

Snyder, Francis, 'Soft Law and Institutional Practice in the European Community', in Stephen Martin (ed), *The Construction of Europe: Essays in Honour of Emile Noël* (Kluwer, 1994).

Solis, Gary D, *The Law of Armed Conflict: International Humanitarian Law in War* (3rd ed, Cambridge University Press, 2022).

Stapleton-Coory, Mitchell, 'The Enduring Legacy of the Martens Clause: Resolving the Conflict of Morality in International Humanitarian Law' (2019) 40 *Adelaide Law Review* 471.

State Council Information Office of the People's Republic of China, *China's National Defense in the New Era* (July 2019), https://english.www.gov.cn/archive/whitepaper/201907/24/content_WS5d3941ddc6d08408f502283d.html.

Stoutland, Page O, and Samantha Pitts-Kiefer, 'Nuclear Weapons in the New Cyber Age: Report of the Cyber-Nuclear Weapons Study Group' (*Nuclear Threat Initiative*, September 2018), www.nti.org/analysis/articles/nuclear-weapons-cyber-age/.

Sundaram, Kumar, and MV Ramana, 'India and the Policy of No First Use of Nuclear Weapons' (2018) 1 *Journal for Peace and Nuclear Disarmament* 152.

Swiss Federal Department of Foreign Affairs, Directorate of International Law, *Expert Meeting of Governmental and Other Experts on Private Military and Security Companies*, 13–14 November 2006, Montreux, Chair's Summary (22 July 2007).

Swiss Federal Department of Foreign Affairs, Directorate of International Law, *Workshop of Governmental Experts and Industry Representatives on Private Military/Security Companies*, 16–17 January 2006, Zurich, Summary of the Chair (1 September 2006).

Take, Ingo, 'Legitimacy in Global Governance: International, Transnational and Private Institutions Compared' (2012) 18 *Swiss Political Science Review* 220.

Tammes, AJP, 'Soft Law', in TMC Asser Institute (ed), *Essays on International & Comparative Law in Honour of Judge Erades* (Martinus Nijhoff Publishers, 1983).

Thomas, AR, and James C Duncan (eds), *Annotated Supplement to the Commander's Handbook on the Law of Naval Operations*, reprinted in *International Law Studies*, vol 73 (Naval War College, 1999).

TOI Staff, 'Israeli Jets Said to Strike Iranian-Run Missile Production Facility in Syria', *Times of Israel* (22 July 2018), www.timesofisrael.com/israel-jets-said-to-strike-chemical-weapons-site-in-syria/.

Tougas, Marie-Louise, 'Some Comments and Observations on the Montreux Document' (2009) 12 *Yearbook of International Humanitarian Law* 312.

Turkish National Commission of Inquiry, *Report on the Israeli Attack on the Humanitarian Aid Convoy to Gaza on 31 May 2010* (Turkish National Commission of Inquiry, February 2011).

Tzouvala, Ntina, 'The "Unwilling or Unable" Doctrine and the Political Economy of the War on Terror' (2023) 14 *Humanity* 19.

Unal, Beyza, and Patricia Lewis, 'Cybersecurity of Nuclear Weapons Systems: Threats, Vulnerabilities, and Consequences' (*Chatham House*, January 2018), https://stanleycenter.org/publications/cybersecurity-of-nuclear-weapons-systems-threats-vulnerabilities-and-consequences/.

United Kingdom, *Parliamentary Debates* (Hansard), House of Lords, 30 October 2012, vol 740, col 495.

United Kingdom Defence Nuclear Organisation and Ministry of Defence, 'Dreadnought Submarine Programme: Factsheet' (16 March 2021), www.gov.uk/government/publications/successor-submarine-programme-factsheet/successor-submarine-programme-factsheet.

United Kingdom Defence Nuclear Organisation and Ministry of Defence, 'UK's Nuclear Deterrent (CASD)' (16 March 2021), www.gov.uk/government/collections/uks-nuclear-deterrent-casd.

United Kingdom Government, 'Integrated Review of Security, Defence, Development and Foreign Policy 2021: Nuclear Deterrent' (17 March 2021), www.gov.uk/guidance/integrated-review-of-security-defence-development-and-foreign-policy-2021-nuclear-deterrent.

United Kingdom Government, 'Integrated Review Refresh 2023: Responding to a More Contested and Volatile World' (March 2023), https://assets.publishing.service.gov.uk/government/uploads/system/uploads/attachment_data/file/1145586/11857435_NS_IR_Refresh_2023_Supply_AllPages_Revision_7_WEB_PDF.pdf.

United Kingdom Government, *Securing Britain in an Age of Uncertainty: The Strategic Defence and Security Review* (HM Government, October 2010).

United Kingdom Ministry of Defence, *The Joint Service Manual of the Law of Armed Conflict* (JSP 383, 2004).

United Kingdom Secretary of State, Ministry of Defence, Letter to Rt Hon James Arbuthnot MP, on the Ministry's approach toward private security companies (12 May 2014), www.parliament.uk/documents/commons-committees/defence/140512-SoS-to-Chair-re-Private-Security-Companies.pdf.

United Nations, 'Despite Progress, Civilians Continue to Bear Brunt of Conflict, Says Under-Secretary-General in Briefing to Security Council', UN Meetings Coverage and Press Releases, Security Council, 6151st Meeting, UN Doc SC/9692 (26 June 2009), https://press.un.org/en/2009/sc9692.doc.htm.

United Nations, *Documents of the United Nations Conference on International Organization, San Francisco, 1945: Volume III* (United Nations Information Organizations, 1945).

United Nations, 'Flouting International Law, Racism Pervades All Countries, Third Committee Hears at Start of Debate', UN Meetings Coverage and

Press Releases, General Assembly, Sixty-ninth Session, 37th & 38th Meetings, UN Doc GA/SHC/4115 (3 November 2014), https://press.un.org/en/2014/gashc4115.doc.htm.

United Nations, 'In Presidential Statement, Security Council Reaffirms Commitment to Protection of Civilians in Armed Conflict, Adopts Updated Aide Memoire on Issue', UN Meetings Coverage and Press Releases, Security Council, 6427th Meeting, UN Doc SC/10089 (22 November 2010), www.un.org/unispal/document/auto-insert-207387/.

United Nations, 'Member States', www.un.org/en/about-us/member-states.

United Nations, 'Mongolia's Nuclear-Weapon-Free Status', www.un.org/nwfz/content/mongolias-nuclear-weapon-free-status.

United Nations, *A More Secure World: Our Shared Responsibility, Report of the High-Level Panel on Threats, Challenges and Change* (United Nations, 2004).

United Nations, 'Non-Member States', www.un.org/en/about-us/non-member-states).

United Nations, *Report of the Conference of the Committee on Disarmament: Volume I*, General Assembly, Official Records, Thirty-first Session, Supplement No 27, UN Doc A/31/27 (1976), https://digitallibrary.un.org/record/697097.

United Nations, *Report of the United Nations Conference on Environment and Development*, vol I, UN Doc A/CONF.151/26 (1993).

United Nations, 'Responsibility of States to Ensure Protection of Diplomatic Personnel, Premises Is Reviewed by Assembly's Legal Committee', UN Meetings Coverage and Press Releases, General Assembly, Sixty-fifth General Assembly, Sixth Committee, 13th & 14th Meetings, UN Doc GA/L/3394 (18 October 2010), https://press.un.org/en/2010/gal3394.doc.htm.

United Nations Committee Against Torture and Other Cruel, Inhuman or Degrading Treatment or Punishment, *List of Issues in Connection with the Consideration of the Fifth Periodic Report of the United Kingdom of Great Britain and Northern Ireland, Adopted by the Committee at Its Forty-ninth Session (29 October–23 November 2012)*, UN Doc CAT/C/GBR/Q/5/Add.1 (2 May 2013).

United Nations Committee on the Peaceful Uses of Outer Space, *Voluntary Implementation of the Guidelines for the Long-term Sustainability of Outer Space Activities: Report by Italy*, UN Doc A/AC.105/C.1/2023/CRP.11 (6 February 2023).

United Nations Committee on the Rights of the Child, *Consideration of Reports Submitted by States Parties Under Article 8 of the Optional Protocol to the Convention on the Rights of Child on Involvement of Children in Armed Conflict: Initial Reports of States Parties Due in 2008 – Slovakia [30 October 2009]*, UN Doc CRC/C/OPAC/SVK/1 (14 June 2011).

United Nations Committee on the Rights of the Child, *Consideration of Reports Submitted by States Parties Under Article 8(1) of the Optional Protocol to the Convention on the Rights of the Child on the Involvement of Children in Armed Conflict: Initial Reports of States Parties Due in 2008 – Slovakia*, UN Doc CRC/C/OPAC/SVK/1 (13 May 2011).

United Nations Department of Safety and Security, *United Nations Security Management System: Security Policy Manual* (UNDSS, 2011).

United Nations General Assembly, *Letter Dated 22 August 1996 from the Permanent Representative of Australia to the United Nations Addressed to the Secretary-General*, UN Doc A/50/1027 (26 August 1996).

United Nations General Assembly, *Note Verbale Dated 26 July 2016 from the Permanent Mission of Croatia to the United Nations Addressed to the President of the General Assembly*, UN Doc A/71/225 (28 July 2016).

United Nations General Assembly, *Note Verbale Dated 26 October 2016 from the Permanent Mission of the United States of America to the United Nations Addressed to the President of the General Assembly*, UN Doc A/71/585 (31 October 2016).

United Nations General Assembly, *Resolution 33/71 B: Non-Use of Nuclear Weapons and Prevention of Nuclear War*, UN Doc A/RES/33/71[B] (14 December 1978).

United Nations General Assembly, *Resolution 34/83 G: Non-Use of Nuclear Weapons and Prevention of Nuclear War*, UN Doc A/RES/34/83[G] (11 December 1979).

United Nations General Assembly, *Resolution 35/152 D: Non-Use of Nuclear Weapons and Prevention of Nuclear War*, UN Doc A/RES/35/152[D] (12 December 1980).

United Nations General Assembly, *Resolution 36/92 I: Non-Use of Nuclear Weapons and Prevention of Nuclear War*, UN Doc A/RES/36/92[I] (9 December 1981).

United Nations General Assembly, *Resolution 45/59 B: Convention on the Prohibition of the Use of Nuclear Weapons*, UN Doc A/RES/45/59[B] (4 December 1990).

United Nations General Assembly, *Resolution 46/37 D: Convention on the Prohibition of the Use of Nuclear Weapons*, UN Doc A/RES/46/37[D] (6 December 1991).

United Nations General Assembly, *Resolution 49/75 K: Request for an Advisory Opinion from the International Court of Justice on the Legality of the Threat or Use of Nuclear Weapons*, UN Doc A/RES/49/75[K] (15 December 1994).

United Nations General Assembly, *Resolution 50/245: Comprehensive Nuclear-Test-Ban Treaty*, UN Doc A/RES/50/245 (17 September 1996).

United Nations General Assembly, *Resolution 59/91: The Hague Code of Conduct Against Ballistic Missile Proliferation*, UN Doc A/RES/59/91 (17 December 2004).

United Nations General Assembly, *Resolution 77/58: The Hague Code of Conduct Against Ballistic Missile Proliferation* UN Doc A/RES/77/58 (14 December 2022).

United Nations General Assembly, *Resolution 217A (III): Universal Declaration of Human Rights*, UN Doc A/RES/217(III) (10 December 1948).

United Nations General Assembly, *Resolution 1514 (XV): Declaration on the Granting of Independence to Colonial Countries and Peoples*, UN Doc A/RES/1514(XV) (14 December 1960).

United Nations General Assembly, *Resolution 1653 (XVI): Declaration on the Prohibition of the Use of Nuclear and Thermo-Nuclear Weapons*, UN Doc A/RES/1653(XVI) (24 November 1961).

United Nations General Assembly, *Resolution 2131 (XX): Declaration on the Inadmissibility of Intervention in the Domestic Affairs of States and the Protection of Their Independence and Sovereignty*, UN Doc A/RES/2131(XX) (21 December 1965).

United Nations General Assembly, *Resolution 2444 (XXIII): Respect for Human Rights in Armed Conflicts*, UN Doc A/RES/2444(XXIII) (19 December 1968).

United Nations General Assembly, *Resolution 2625 (XXV): Declaration on Principles of International Law Concerning Friendly Relations and Co-operation Among States in Accordance with the Charter of the United Nations*, UN Doc 2625 (XXV) (24 October 1970).

United Nations General Assembly, *Resolution 3314 (XXIX): Definition of Aggression*, UN Doc A/RES/3314(XXIX) (14 December 1974).

United Nations General Assembly, *Use of Mercenaries as a Means of Violating Human Rights and Impeding the Exercise of the Right of Peoples to Self-Determination: Note by the Secretary-General*, UN Doc A/77/268 (4 August 2022).

United Nations General Assembly and Security Council, *Letter Dated 2 October 2008 from the Permanent Representative of Switzerland to the United Nations Addressed to the Secretary-General*, UN Doc A/63/467–S/2008/636 (6 October 2008).

United Nations General Assembly Sixth Committee, *Summary Record of the 15th Meeting*, UN Doc A/C.6/69/SR.15 (2 December 2014).

United Nations Human Rights Committee, *Consideration of Reports Submitted by States Parties Under Article 40 of the Covenant, Fourth Periodic Report: United States of America [30 December 2011]*, UN Doc CCPR/C/USA/4 (22 May 2012).

United Nations Human Rights Committee, *General Comment No 36 on Article 6: Right to Life*, UN Doc CCPR/C/GC/36 (3 September 2019).

United Nations Human Rights Council, *Implementation of General Assembly Resolution 60/251 of 15 March 2006 Entitled 'Human Rights Council': Report of the Commission of Inquiry on Lebanon Pursuant to Human Rights Council Resolution S-2/1*, UN Doc A/HRC/3/2 (23 November 2006).

United Nations Human Rights Council, *Promotion and Protection of All Human Rights, Civil, Political, Economic, Social and Cultural Rights, Including the Right to Development: Report of the Working Group on the Use of Mercenaries as a Means of Violating Human Rights and Impeding the Exercise of the Right of Peoples to Self-Determination*, UN Doc A/HRC/10/14 (21 January 2009).

United Nations Human Rights Council, *Report of the International Fact-Finding Mission to Investigate Violations of International Law, Including International Humanitarian and Human Rights Law, Resulting from the Israeli Attacks on the Flotilla of Ships Carrying Humanitarian Assistance*, UN Doc A/HRC/15/21 (27 September 2010).

United Nations Human Rights Council, *Report of the Open-Ended Intergovernmental Working Group to Consider the Possibility of Elaborating an International Regulatory Framework on the Regulation, Monitoring and Oversight of the Activities of Private Military and Security Companies on Its Second Session*, UN Doc A/HRC/22/41 (24 December 2012).

United Nations Human Rights Council, *Report of the Open-Ended Intergovernmental Working Group to Consider the Possibility of Elaborating an International Regulatory Framework on the Regulation, Monitoring and Oversight of the Activities of Private Military and Security Companies on Its Fourth Session*, UN Doc A/HRC/30/47 (9 July 2015).
United Nations Human Rights Council, *Report of the Working Group on the Use of Mercenaries as a Means of Violating Human Rights and Impeding the Exercise of the Right of Peoples to Self-Determination*, UN Doc A/HRC/15/25 (5 July 2010).
United Nations Human Rights Council, *Report of the Working Group on the Use of Mercenaries as a Means of Violating Human Rights and Impeding the Exercise of the Right of Peoples to Self-Determination: Mission to Ghana (8 to 15 December 2017)*, UN Doc A/HRC/39/49/Add.1 (7 December 2018).
United Nations Human Rights Council, *Summary of the First Session of the Open-Ended Intergovernmental Working Group to Consider the Possibility of Elaborating an International Regulatory Framework on the Regulation, Monitoring and Oversight of the Activities of Private Military and Security Companies*, UN Doc A/HRC/WG.10/1/4 (22 November 2011).
United Nations Human Rights Council, *Summary of the Third Session of the Open-Ended Intergovernmental Working Group to Consider the Possibility of Elaborating an International Regulatory Framework on the Regulation, Monitoring and Oversight of the Activities of Private Military and Security Companies*, UN Doc A/HRC/WG.10/3/2 (2 September 2014).
United Nations Office for the Coordination of Humanitarian Affairs, *Oxford Guidance on the Law Relating to Humanitarian Relief Operations in Situations of Armed Conflict* (OCHA, 2016).
United Nations Office on Drugs and Crime, *State Regulation Concerning Civilian Private Security Services and Their Contribution to Crime Prevention and Security Safety* (UNODC, 2014).
United Nations Secretary-General, *In Larger Freedom: Towards Development, Security and Human Rights for All*, UN Doc A/59/2005 (21 March 2005).
United Nations Security Council, 'Better Control of Borders, Private Security Firms Key to Stopping "Guns for Hire", Speakers Say at Security Council Debate on Mercenary Activities in Africa', UN Meetings Coverage and Press Releases, 8456th Meeting, UN Doc SC/13688 (4 February 2019), https://press.un.org/en/2019/sc13688.doc.htm.
United Nations Security Council, *Comments by Poland, France, Germany, the United Kingdom, and South Africa*, UN Doc S/PV.8456 (4 February 2019).
United Nations Security Council, *Conflict-Related Sexual Violence: Report of the Secretary-General*, UN Doc S/2023/413 (22 June 2023).
United Nations Security Council, *Letter Dated 8 March 2021 from the Permanent Representative of Mexico to the United Nations Addressed to the President of the Security Council*, UN Doc S/2021/247 (16 March 2021), annex I.
United Nations Security Council, *Letter from the Permanent Representative of the Russian Federation to the United Nations Addressed to the Secretary-General*, UN Doc S/2022/154 (24 February 2022).

United Nations Security Council, *Meeting Records, 6151st Meeting*, Statement by the Permanent Representative of Mexico, UN Doc S/PV.6151 (26 June 2009).
United Nations Security Council, *Resolution 1368*, UN Doc S/RES/1368 (12 September 2001).
United Nations Security Council, *Resolution 1373*, UN Doc S/RES/1373 (28 September 2011).
United States, *National Security Strategy of the United States* (The White House, December 2017).
United States Air Force, *Air Force Nuclear Command, Control, and Communications (NC3)*, Air Force Instruction 13–550 (16 April 2019), https://static.e-publishing.af.mil/production/1/af_a10/publication/afi13-550/afi13-550.pdf.
United States Department of Defense, '2022 National Defense Strategy of the United States of America' (October 2022), https://media.defense.gov/2022/Oct/27/2003103845/-1/-1/1/2022-NATIONAL-DEFENSE-STRATEGY-NPR-MDR.PDF#page=33.
United States Department of Defense, 'Law of War Manual' (June 2015, updated July 2023).
United States Department of Defense, 'Nuclear Posture Review 2018' (February 2018), https://media.defense.gov/2018/feb/02/2001872877/-1/-1/1/executive-summary.pdf.
United States Department of Defense, 'Nuclear Posture Review 2022' (2022), https://media.defense.gov/2022/Oct/27/2003103845/-1/-1/1/2022-NATIONAL-DEFENSE-STRATEGY-NPR-MDR.PDF.
United States Department of State, 'Missile Technology Control Regime (MTCR) Frequently Asked Questions: Fact Sheet' (2025), www.state.gov/bureau-of-international-security-and-nonproliferation/releases/2025/01/missile-technology-control-regime-mtcr-frequently-asked-questions.
United States Department of State, 'P3 Joint Statement on Security Assurances' (4 August 2022), https://2021-2025.state.gov/p3-joint-statement-on-security-assurances/.
United States Department of State, 'Treaty for the Prohibition of Nuclear Weapons in Latin America and the Caribbean (Treaty of Tlatelolco)', https://2009-2017.state.gov/t/isn/4796.htm.
United States Department of State, Office of the Historian, 'The Australia, New Zealand and United States Security Treaty (ANZUS Treaty), 1951', https://history.state.gov/milestones/1945-1952/anzus.
United States Navy, United States Marine Corps, and United States Coast Guard, *The Commander's Handbook on The Law of Naval Operations* (NWP 1–14M, MCTP 11–10B, COMDTPUB P5800.7A, March 2022).
Vaish, Varun, 'Negotiating the India-Pakistan Conflict in Relation to Kashmir' (2011) 28 *International Journal on World Peace* 53.
Van Diepen, Vann H, 'Origins and Development of the Hague Code of Conduct' (*HCoC Research Papers*, No 11, October 2022), www.nonproliferation.eu/hcoc/wp-content/uploads/2022/10/Origins-of-the-Code.pdf.
Wallace, David A, 'International Code of Conduct for Private Security Service Providers' (2011) 50 *International Legal Materials* 89.

Waseem, Rubina, 'Flux in the Middle East and Nuclear Israel' (2020) 6 *Journal of Security and Strategic Analyses* 55.

Watkin, Kenneth, 'Opportunity Lost: Organised Armed Groups and the ICRC "Direct Participation in Hostilities" Interpretive Guidance' (2010) 42 *New York University Journal of International Law and Politics* 641.

Watson, Darius, 'Rethinking the US Nuclear Triad' (2017) 11 *Strategic Studies Quarterly* 134.

Wellerstein, Alex, 'NC3 Decision Making: Individual Versus Group Process' (*NAPSNet Special Reports*, 8 August 2019), https://nautilus.org/napsnet/napsnet-special-reports/nc3-decision-making-individual-versus-group-process/.

Wilmshurst, Elizabeth, 'Principles of International Law on the Use of Force by States in Self-Defence' (*Chatham House*, ILP WP 05/01, Royal Institute of International Affairs, 2005).

Wilson, Robert Samuel, and Russell Rumbaugh, 'Reversal of Nuclear-Conventional Entanglement in Outer Space' (2024) 47 *Journal of Strategic Studies* 64.

Wirtz, James J, and Jeffrey A Larsen (eds), *Nuclear Command, Control, and Communications: A Primer on US Systems and Future Challenges* (Georgetown University Press, 2022).

Wolfrum, Rüdiger, 'Legitimacy of International Law from a Legal Perspective: Some Introductory Considerations', in Rüdiger Wolfrum and Volker Röben (eds), *Legitimacy in International Law* (Springer, 2008).

Zamir, Noam, 'The Distinction Between International and Non-International Armed Conflicts', in *Classification of Conflicts in International Humanitarian Law: The Legal Impact of Foreign Intervention in Civil Wars* (Edward Elgar, 2017).

Zaum, Dominik, 'Legitimacy', in Jacob Katz Cogan, Ian Hurd, and Ian Johnstone (eds), *The Oxford Handbook of International Organizations* (Oxford University Press, 2016).

Index

Note: page numbers in **bold** indicate a table on the corresponding page.

For Product Safety Concerns and Information please contact our
EU representative GPSR@taylorandfrancis.com Taylor & Francis
Verlag GmbH, Kaufingerstraße 24, 80331 München, Germany